THE AMERICAN NIGHTMARE AND THE ART OF FAILURE

THE AMERICAN NIGHTMARE AND THE ART OF FAILURE

Life with PTSD

MATTHEW ALTOBELLI

THE AMERICAN NIGHTMARE AND THE ART OF FAILURE
LIFE WITH PTSD

iUniverse books may be ordered through booksellers or by contacting:

iUniverse
1663 Liberty Drive
Bloomington, IN 47403
www.iuniverse.com
1-800-Authors (1-800-288-4677)

ISBN: 978-1-5320-6440-1 (sc)
ISBN: 978-1-5320-6439-5 (hc)
ISBN: 978-1-5320-6438-8 (e)

Library of Congress Control Number: 2018914837

Print information available on the last page.

iUniverse rev. date: 12/19/2018

This book is dedicated to my family, Amanda, Morgan, Sean, Henry, my parents, and all the friends and enemies I have made that had to deal with my illness. It is also dedicated to all those who suffer, and those we lost to the suffering.

1. **General Disclaimer**

1.1 The views expressed in this memoir are for educational uses only and should not be taken as medical advice. They are the accounts of one person's experience, and your experience may differ. If you are in need of help, please contact a medical professional.

1.2 Some names and identifying features have been purposely omitted to protect their identity.

2. **No advice**

2.1 contains general medical information.

2.2 The medical information is not advice and should not be treated as such.

3. **No warranties**

3.1 The medical information is provided without any representations or warranties, express or implied.

3.2 Without limiting the scope of Section 3.1, we do not warrant or represent that the medical information:

(a) will be constantly available, or available at all; or

(b) is true, accurate, complete, current or non-misleading.

4. **Medical assistance**

4.1 You must not rely on the information as an alternative to medical advice from your doctor or other professional healthcare provider.

4.2 If you have any specific questions about any medical matter, you should consult your doctor or other professional healthcare provider.

4.3 If you think you may be suffering from any medical condition, you should seek immediate medical attention.

4.4 You should never delay seeking medical advice, disregard medical advice or discontinue medical treatment.

a kindhearted person. I am not so sure that is what it's all about. Part of me believes that it is to make up for a past that I no longer want to remember. To make things right. To somehow make it up to God for all the wrong I have done. All the mistakes I have made, and all the people I have hurt.

This is my story. How I became the way I am, and how I am trying to become the person I want to be. With the work that I do, and have done, I have met so many people. I have listened to the stories of their lives. I have built relationships with them. What this has taught me is that people are not really any different from one another. We all seek peace. We all seek happiness. We all seek acceptance. Everyone has a different definition of those words though, and that is where things get messy. We use the excuse "I'm only human" to own up to our mistakes. As if that phrase is a get out of jail free card, and our actions are acceptable because we are only human. I dedicate my story, my struggle, to the people suffering from PTSD and looking for success. I know how hard it is to find.

I hope that you will learn from my failures on my path to success and be able to recognize them in your own life so you can avoid the place where I ended up. The events and "episodes" that followed have caused me to examine the human mind and ask some tough questions. If PTSD is an illness, can it be cured? What is the root cause for why we act the way we do? Is it a single event that triggers the disorder, or a culmination of events in our lives that overwhelm our psyche? As I search through my experiences for what caused my brain to operate the way it does, I found one thing to be true. It all started with a picture. To those who suffer, and the ones who watch the suffering, this is for you.

PART 1
ACQUIRED

Chapter 1

TRIGGER

"Okay airman, let's take this from the top. I need the details of what happened." the agent from the Office of Special Investigations (OSI) said to me as he gestured to the chair in front of me.

I pulled out the chair and sat down, staring blankly right through him. Sitting in a dark lit room, around 0400, the man before me looked tired; he had a prominent five-o'clock shadow, and dark circles under his eyes. His face gave off a vibe that he didn't want to be there, and he didn't want to spend too much time with me. I tried to recall the events that just took place but found myself at a loss for words. The smell of iron from the blood soaking into the Afghan soil still fresh in my nose. The loud bang of my M16 as it released the ammo caused a flash that would imprint a picture of that moment in my brain forever. A photograph that I could recall at any moment like I had it saved on my phone or in a scrapbook. The look of fear on the three men's face as they realized this would be the last day of their lives. A picture with a dark backdrop, blood in the foreground, and regret as the immediate emotion that comes to mind when recalling this picture. The world around this 20-foot radius had disappeared, and only this picture had survived the flash.

"Kid, I know it's been a rough night for you, but I need you to help me out so I can help you out. So again, what happened?" The OSI agent said to me, seemingly frustrated that I had not answered him yet.

"Yes, sir. I will try." I answered him.

The year was 2007, and I was at Bagram Air Field in a Valley surrounded by mountains in Afghanistan. I was a 19-year-old kid and terrified at the events that preceded this interrogation. Where do I even begin to explain how this came to pass? I started to recall the events of the day, so I could tell them to the Agent. It was a Tuesday, my crews only day off. It was dark. The middle of the night due to my shift being from 6pm until 6am. I attempted to keep my sleep schedule on my days off, so I stayed up all night. On Tuesdays, you could usually find me at the gym, and then I would head to midnight chow, eat, and then spend the rest of my night watching movies on my laptop that were shared among the other members of my deployment. I must have watched a bootleg copy of "Superbad" about twenty or thirty times while I was in Afghanistan. It was this fateful night though that I was missing home.

I hadn't talked to my father for a while, so I thought I would walk down to the phone area by the bazaar and make a call. It was about 3am. I checked into my wingman's bunk to see if he wanted to go with me, but he was asleep. I grabbed my M16 and slung it around my back. I did not always have it slung around my back, but It was more comfortable, so tonight I did. I slung it around my back. I slung it around my back. I slung it around my back. I feel like if I had it slung in front of me, most of what happened next would not have gone down how it did.

I started to head for the Phone booths down at the Bazar. We had one in our maintenance bay that I had used a dozen times before. I don't know why I decided not to use it this night. I think because it was a beautiful, calm night, and I wanted to take a walk. The Stars in Afghanistan were always so bright. There were no city lights, or tall buildings to take away from their shimmer. I would often sit on a bench we had built when there was nothing to do and star gaze. I would always see Orion's Belt so easily from there. The nighttime air was refreshing on my skin and offered an escape from the heat of the Afghanistan sun. The sun would rise at around 5am each day, and it was a beautiful sight to watch it come up over the mountains. Afghanistan had a lot of natural beauty to it. It is something that you don't often hear about because of the chaotic political state of the Middle East. I always thought of the area as serene during the night.

Now my trip to the phones can only be described as the calm before the storm. 3am in Afghanistan meant it was almost 3pm back in New York. If I ever wanted to reach my family at home, I would need to call them in the middle of the night my time, or early morning before they had gone to bed. The conversations were never that long because other people wanted to make calls too, and we only had so many minutes on our calling cards. I would call my Grandpa and Nana to make sure they knew I was ok, and my mother and father. I would call my wife, Alyssa to find out how she was doing and get any updates on her pregnancy. We were expecting a little girl.

I made it to the area where the phone booth was. The way it was set up was you had to turn a corner at the Post exchange (PX), and the booth was in the middle of an open area with other crates stacked up to the left of it. The crates were lined up so you could walk between them. Once you turned the corner and the booth was visible, you had about 50 more yards to walk before you got to the booth. The booth and crates on the left were apparent as soon as you turned the corner. I started walking towards the booth and took maybe ten steps before I stopped abruptly. I froze, trying to process what I was seeing and how I would proceed. I looked past the phone booth to the crates on the left and noticed three Afghani nationals, which we called TCNs (Third Country Nationals). As soon as I stopped, they looked at me.

Many of the day to day tasks on the base was done by TCNs. They would clean out the port-a-johns, and work in the chow hall or be responsible for getting our laundry done. They would also do some construction work on base, like pavement or patching up potholes. TCNs were always accompanied by a member of our military. These three men had no escort. Immediately I felt like something was wrong. This moment seemed to last forever. A lot went through my head. What are they doing here? Why are they on base right now? Where is their escort? What should I do? It was night, and the area was not well lit. There were about 40 Yards between us now.

They saw me, and I saw them. My weapon was slung around my back. My weapon was slung around my back. My weapon was slung around my back. I believe the TCN's assessed the situation and thought I was unarmed. They were unarmed, and began to run. Not away from me, but at me. I now felt a surge of adrenalin and whipped my M16 from my back up to a firing position. I pulled the charging handle and chambered a round while simultaneously switching my weapon from safe to fire with my thumb. I shouted, "stop!" The men now about 10 yards away began to slow down. It did not matter to me. Maybe I hadn't been able to process the fact that they were slowing down and possibly stopping at the moment. I will never know. In my explanation to the OSI agent, I decided to omit this information as I could see it harming me. The fact is I was young and scared and wanted the threat to be neutralized.

I squeezed the trigger and hit the fastest one. The one closest to me, and he went down. I quickly moved my firearm to the second one and squeezed the trigger two more times, he went down. The third guy was now sliding and falling trying to stop himself. He was on the ground, and I pointed my firearm at him and unloaded a few rounds hitting him a couple times. He seemed to have died instantly. The second guy I hit looked to be unconscious. The first one had his eyes open. He was looking at me and did not talk. I had hit him in the chest and believe I punctured a lung. I just watched him die. His blood ran and seeped into the ground. It wasn't just the visual that stuck with me. The smell of my recently discharged firearm, mixed with the iron-like smell of blood and sand is also something imprinted on my mind. The cold night's air of Afghanistan which once offered relief from the heat now had no effect on me as my body reached a boiling point. The stars that once gave me comfort at night had gone dim.

I stood there, put my weapon back on safe and slung it around my back. The noise from the gunshots was sure to draw some attention, and before I knew it, security forces had arrived. I stood over the seemingly lifeless bodies as a few trucks of Security forces members swarmed around me. I felt relieved to see them because I had no idea what to do. They exited their vehicles and what happened next confused me. They pointed their weapons at me and ordered me to drop to my knees. I complied. They ordered me to raise my hands and spread my fingers. I complied. One of the men came up from behind me and disarmed me, then followed it up with his knee in my back and violently putting me on my face and restraining me. More confusion set in. Was I the enemy? I believe at that moment my body went into a state of shock because the next thing I remember I was in a dark lit room staring at an OSI agent who was asking me questions.

"That's all I know. What happened is still a little confusing to me. Can I go?" I asked him

"Not yet. Hang tight for a few minutes. I will be right back."

He exited the room and left me to my own devices. The restraints had been removed, and I no longer felt like a prisoner, yet I certainly didn't feel free. In fact, I did not feel much of anything. Where did he go? What was he doing? What was going to happen next? A few minutes turned into an hour, maybe longer. I did not know because there was no clock in this room. Also, at this point time was irrelevant. I had no desire to leave the room. I do not mean at this moment, but ever. As the realization of what had occurred hit me, I thought that outside of this room I would have to face what I have done. I would need to process it and deal with it. It would become real. People would be around me, and I would need to go on living as if I was still normal. Inside this room I was alone. I could be alone and never have to explain myself to anyone. I wanted to be alone forever because it was easier than dealing with it. This was the night the monster inside of me came into creation. Much like a human child, it would need time to grow and develop, but this was the start of something much worse.

"Ok Airman, we need to talk," he said as he re-entered the room.

"Yes, Sir."

"What happened today was clearly in self-defense, correct?" He waited as I nodded "However, it was against three men who worked for the base. These were people hired by the government to do a Job. There are hundreds of others like them. This is where the situation gets a little sticky."

"What do you mean?" I said, now feeling worried that I would need to be made an example of.

"Imagine if you will, the rest of the force learning what happened tonight? The people who work in the kitchen, the ones cleaning and doing laundry, all TCNs like the men you gunned down tonight. Now imagine if everyone suddenly didn't trust them anymore? What do you think that would do to this base?"

"I'm not sure I understand," I said

"To make this interaction short, the commander has decided that tonight's events stay classified. Do you know what that means, son?"

I stared blankly back at him.

"It means we can't talk about it. To anyone. Do you know the penalty for releasing classified information?"

"Yes, sir."

"Ok good. Off the record, I just want to say I am sorry for how this all went down tonight. You were very brave. I just have a little more paperwork to do, and then we are going to send you over to the hospital to get checked out."

I did not feel brave. In fact, I feel like what I did was the opposite of bravery. I was scared, and I fired my weapon to save my own life. At that moment I was not thinking about anyone else on the base, or my country, or the uniform I wore. I was just thinking about my life, and how I did not want it to end. The irony of this was after the fact, I no longer cared if it ended. I sat in the room again, alone, with my thoughts and waited to be escorted to the hospital. I was not sure why they were sending me there. I was not hit, I was physically ok. They were not checking me out for my physical health though. They wanted to make sure I was mentally fit enough to go back to work and carry a firearm.

A member of security forces came and got me and walked me outside. The sun was up now, and the base was bustling with soldiers, airman, and marines all running around and heading to their duty stations. The air was beginning to become hot, as the summer mornings heat up quick in Afghanistan, often reaching near 100 degrees by noon. I walked with the security forces member to the hospital which was not far from where I was being detained. I wondered if this airman knew what had happened or if he was there earlier. Maybe he was the one who disarmed me and shoved me into the ground. I did not ask. I did not say anything to him. We arrived at the hospital, and he handed me off and went about his way.

I would need to miss work, so they told me to tell my unit I got food poisoning from eating a lousy sub from the Subway on base. Yes, we had a Subway, and a Burger King, and KFC and even a Pizzahut on base. Sounds good right? It wasn't the same, and I only ate it a couple of times before giving up on the idea that anything in this country could taste like or remind me of home. The squadron gave me the days I needed to recover. I am not sure if my commander was filled in on what had happened or if anyone was running interference on this because they kept me in the dark. The Doctors evaluated me for injury and then assessed my mental stability. I was always good at telling people what they wanted to hear so I could go about my life uninterrupted. I probably should have been more honest with them, but I was scared about what would happen to me. I did not want to lose my job, or worse.

As far as war stories go, this one is not very exciting. It didn't involve some big mission and would likely make a terrible movie if anyone ever put it into film, but for me it was traumatic. It may not sound like a big deal, because of how our media is and the fact that killing and death seems to be a regular part of life now, but I was not born a killer. I don't have the will to hurt or kill anyone. I understand the irony of this because I was a weapons troop and realize that my actions led to the death of thousands, but if I could not see them die, I could tell myself that it was only bad people, and we were doing good deeds over in the Middle East. It was easy to lie to myself about what was going on if I didn't actually see it happen, but when you are in the middle of it, it becomes real. At that moment I was not fighting for my country. I was not fighting for glory, or for my brothers or sisters. I was there, all alone, and I was struggling to survive. Maybe it would have been different if I was with another Airman. If my wingman was awake and came with me, but the fact was, it was just me, and I needed to live.

I was given my weapon back, with the expended ammo now back in my clip and sent back to my RLB (Relocatable building). I sat in my bunk, laid down and tried to sleep. Trauma mixed with malaria medication is a deadly mental poison. The drug already induced vivid nightmares, but now my mind gave it something useful to craft masterpieces of psychological destruction with. I think that is why my brain created a false reality that I tried to believe. One where I walked by the men and just made a phone call. My brain's way of trying to protect me. I wanted to believe that's what happened so bad, and the rest was just an induced nightmare by the medication. My nights were spent worrying now instead of sleeping. I would often just cry. This event shook my trust in people. We were told these people wouldn't hurt us, and they were on our side, but they ran at me. Then upon seeing the "good guys," they apprehended me like I was a war criminal. The next couple of months would be my worst. I would put on a good show at work when I was around people, but then when left alone I would fall apart. If I gave myself an extended amount of time to think I would wander into the world of "what ifs."

What if they had gotten to me? What if they weren't going to attack me? What if they captured me? What if I had used the phone in the maintenance bay? What if I hadn't stopped them? Would more people get hurt? Did I have to kill them? I spent some time watching videos of people dying on the internet. I would look up videos of the Taliban beheading or stabbing Americans because I thought it was a real possibility that any of them could have been me. One of the worst ones I saw was a man having his head pushed on a stone platform. He was being held down by two other men and crying; pleading for his life. A man with a knife walked over to him and thrust the blade into his neck and quickly removed it. The man began to bleed out, and a look of fear came over him. At that moment he knew he was going to die. I wondered what was going through his head as he was dying. What thoughts did the three men who I shot have as they realized they would not survive the night? What would go through my head if I was about to die? It was hard to watch, but I needed to see more. I needed to know that maybe I prevented this from happening. Death became an obsession.

Some nights got the better of me, and I began to go insane. I kept picturing a missile or rocket crashing through the top of my building and blowing me up. I thought of so many ways to die, and the worst thing about them all is I was still alive, waiting for the death I was so certain was coming. A few times I had put the barrel of my M16 in my mouth and took the safety off. The sensation of danger alone was exhilarating. A quick end seemed to be the best way to go. At this moment I realized that time was always irrelevant. One way or another I was going to die. There will come the point in time where I no longer exist in the physical world. Why not end it on my terms? The biggest problem I think is I was alone in this. I could not talk about it with anyone.

So, there it is. The event that would be determined as the cause of my PTSD. I believe there is more to it than this though. To truly understand where we are going and what we become we must analyze where we came from. Killing has been a part of human nature since the dawn of our existence. Why are some men ok with it, and can dissociate their feelings from this, while others plunge into a world filled with nightmares? Do all men suffer this way, and some are just good at hiding it, or are there honestly people out there okay with killing that have no adverse effect on how their mind operates? How do our brains work differently than theirs and why? What is the connection? Maybe we need to look at how we were raised, or what events set the stage for an ultimate diagnosis of PTSD. What events took place that made us classify certain things as trauma when other people don't?

THE BURDEN

I fly up high into the sky
I get shot down and wonder why
I fly up high into the sky
I get shot down but do not cry
This sacrifice I gladly make
This heavy price is mine to take
My fall from heaven, fall from grace
This single tear runs down your face
This world that's turned so very dark
The shadow creeps up through the ark
To take this life, though not in vain
Still it hurts and causes pain
The empty void, a single hole
A place that once you called your soul

I fly up high into the sky
I get shot down and wonder why
I fly up high into the sky
I get shot down but will not lie
The honesty of one man's fate
Is fleeing now through Hell's gate
To take a life for your kin
In Gods eyes is still a sin
A mortal sin we gladly pay
To keep you safe for one more day
And as he fell, you did not shutter
The Oath we took was like no other
The looming threat of impending doom
That we agreed to in that room
Hand held high and voices loud
We had never felt so proud
I fly up high into the sky
I get shot down and wonder why
I fly up high into the sky
I get shot down because I try
Falling faster as I burn
To see your face is all I yearn
One more day, a hand held tight
These are reasons why we fight
The time we had, you'll never know
How it felt to let you go
The land I loved, what it meant to me
This place of dreams I'll never see
A flash of light, my life in trouble
Visions rise now from the rubble
The time we had, I'll always cherish
Now that I'm about to perish

I fly up high into the sky
I get shot down and wonder why
I fly up high into the sky
I get shot down, and now I die
Standing weak, you'll all mourn
And talk of times when I was born
To the world, a name forgotten
Because this planet's become so rotten
To fight for life at any cost
But what's the point when all is lost
As time passes more will vanish
The gates of Hell is where we're banished
The one commandment we have shattered
All for orders we thought mattered
Knowing now how much it hurt
I'd rather be under dirt
Soul still pure and heaven waiting
All the Angels Celebrating
My Return, thy Kingdom come
For all the good that I have done
But instead, it fades to black
For the men that I've sent back
This sacrifice is mine to make
This heavy price is mine to take
So your soul can be pure
All my pain is your cure
I fly up high into the sky
I get shot down, don't wonder why
This life we live is our creation
It comes from all the devastation
When you look for whom to blame
In a mirror, you'll see the same

Chapter 2

PRE-
DETERMINED

Fate. This idea that everything happens for a reason. That even a small event can change the course of your entire future. It can put some people's mind at ease to know that there is a plan set for them, and they are just along for the ride. There are also people who hate the idea of fate because they want to be in control of their lives and every aspect of it. There is no such thing as total control. There will always be outside forces that will toss in the occasional event that you can't control. The small and seemingly insignificant events that happen in our lives that push us ever so gently towards a major life decision like a sailboat out on a lake during a gentle breeze. The destination is determined by the wind, and you can only do so much to steer yourself away from where you are headed. Is it divine intervention, or our own choices?

When people ask me if I had a normal childhood, I don't know how to answer that question. What is a normal childhood?

I don't think I had the best childhood, but I know for a fact I didn't have the worst either. My parents got divorced when I was about seven. I have one brother who is two years younger than I, and a half-sister who is 11 years younger. I have seven stepsisters between my parents. One is my age. Her name is Katie. We were really close as kids, but when we were in 8th grade she had an aneurysm, so, to put my childhood in perspective, I suppose it was pretty average compared to hers. Don't get me wrong, I had my problems too. I was bullied in school and whipped with belts in the gym locker room. I got into fights because I refused to back down and just take it. I was a small, scrawny kid back then, but I could take a beating. I believe that is because of my determination. At the very least, I had heart.

I still maintained good grades, and it wasn't all that apparent that I was struggling in school in a social aspect. It wasn't until things got really bad that my mom decided to move and send me to a different school. Small fights and trouble with students would land me at Athena High School, where I met Alyssa. She was a tall, skinny blonde girl with braces. She was nice to me. Probably one of the few people who were nice to me, so I began to like her. I did make other friends there as well, and pretty quickly. I didn't need to pretend to be someone else either. They liked me for who I was. I made friends with the kid that lived down the street. His name was Greg. Greg and I were into a lot of the same things. We liked the same sports, had the same sense of humor, and liked all the same movies and shows. We seemed pretty identical in almost every way. Except Greg was popular. He had a lot of friends. They soon became my friends, and now I had a group of people that accepted me for who I was.

Alyssa and I soon began to date. We were your typical high school relationship. On again and off again. We would fight and break up only to get back together the next day. This might seem like a typical thing in the world of High School relationships, but it would eventually escalate and become something on a more significant level. We never broke out of this phase in our relationship. Even after we got married, we followed the same pattern. It was toxic to us both. I may have developed a lot of trust issues from this among other things. I often wonder if it was a precursor to why I made the decisions I made on that infamous night in Afghanistan.

The rest of my high school career was pretty standard. I hung out with my friends, played sports, got good grades, and graduated a faceless nobody among the vast population of my school. I was really good at physics. It was probably my best subject. For some reason, my mind could comprehend the physical world and the effects it had on the objects that inhabit it. Now I no longer understand the physical world. Sometimes I am not sure what is real and what is not. For example, during times of high stress, your brain is capable of processing many thoughts all at once, and time seems to slow down. Why does this happen? What does that say about the link between time and the human mind? Does your brain follow the laws of time or even those of the physical world? In extreme cases of trauma and mental illness people can have visual and audio hallucinations, meaning they see things that aren't "really" there, but to them, they are as real as you or me. How powerful is the brain to be able to alter "reality"?

All in all, I had a relatively normal High School experience with events that seemed minor at the time but pushed me on my eventual path to join the Air Force and get married. The first high school I went to, I didn't fit in. I would not do drugs or give in to peer pressure. I was smart, and would not shy away from a fight. This made me a target, and ultimately made up my mom's mind to move me to another school. Greg's friends were friends with a kid, who I would eventually become good friends with. He was joining the Air Force and one day after a conversation with my guidance counselor that didn't go that well he convinced me to come to talk to his recruiter. Also, Athena is where I started dating Alyssa, who I would eventually marry. Butterfly effect. Was it fate? How much control did I really have over these events?

I think the most common and frequent question I have been asked in my existence is "why did you decide to join the military?" to which I usually have some smart ass reply to, such as "I didn't feel like writing an essay to apply for college." Now, obviously that's not true, but I would get a chuckle, and they would forget that I didn't really answer their questions. I could have made up something about New York being my home state, and 9/11 made me very patriotic. Or that I just wanted to serve, or any other cliché answer that military members give. The truth is, I didn't really see any other options for me. Every time I tried to picture my life after High School, I could not see anything. I didn't yet know who I was or what I was supposed to be doing. A conversation with my guidance counselor ultimately made me open up my mind to the Air Force. It was January 2006, and it went a little something like this.

"Matthew Altobelli" The counselor yelled out into the waiting room, as I was next for my senior interview with her. I stood up and walked into her office as she closed the door behind me. I took a seat.

"How are you today, Matthew?" She asked.

"I'm good, how are you?" I replied realizing this was the first interaction I have had with her, and she was supposed to help me figure out what I am going to be doing with my life... No pressure.

"I am good, thank you. I noticed you have not made a decision on where you are going to College yet, is that correct?"

"That's right. I am not sure what I want to do."

"Well, what types of things interest you? Do you have any hobbies?"

I stared blankly at her trying to think about what I liked to do. I tried to think about who I was. It is a hard thing to face when the question is what you want to do for the rest of your life. I was 17 and had no idea.

"Ok Matthew, let's try something else." She said as she began to lay on me all the routine questions a guidance counselor asks to determine what you might be good at or like to do. I believe I stumped her. I will admit, I was pretty hard to talk to back then.

"Well, have you heard of the 2 plus 2 program?"

"Yes, I have" I answered.

"So why don't you sign up for MCC for 2 years, and then you can transfer to a 4-year university to pick and finish up a major you decide you like. That way at least all your core classes are out of the way."

"What if after 2 years I still don't know what I want to do?"

She stared at me with a puzzled look on her face and then smiled.

"Two years is a long time, and you are a smart boy. I am sure you will figure something out."

This was basically a nice way of telling me "Your time is up, and I have other students to see." It did not sit right with me and made my decision to go talk to a recruiter so much easier.

What made it hard to leave was my family and some friends. I was really close with my family and leaving them would prove to be harder than I initially thought. My brother Nick is 22 months younger than me. Almost 2 full years. I had 2 more years on this planet to mess up, and he had 2 years of watching me mess up, so he didn't make the same mistakes I did. Lucky. Speaking of luck, Nick has always had it. He would hit it big at the slots or win things that no one ever wins. He would get away with things that would land you or me in jail. For example, he worked at a bar downtown as a bouncer. The Irony in this is when he was 16 he would drink there using his fake ID. He played in their kickball league, and they would go there after the games. He did look older than 16 because he was really tall, and Italian, so naturally, he could grow facial hair. The funny thing about this is he chose to have his 21st birthday there, which really confused the bartenders and owner who had seen him come in so many times before. So, what do they do? They offer him a job.

Growing up, because we were so close in age, we did a lot together. We were on the same sports teams, we would hang out with the same friends, and we would spend a lot of time outside in our neighborhood. We wouldn't always get along, but for the most part, we did. He was my best friend growing up and is still probably my best friend to this day. He has done a lot for me.

My Next blood sibling is my sister Ryan, or Ryann as she likes to go by now. We have the same mom but different dads. I won't ever call her my half-sister though, because I was there for her since her birth, and she grew up with me. To me, she is my whole sister. Ryann was born on November 27th, 1999. I am 11 years older than her. When she was a baby, she got a lot of attention from everyone. She was my mom's only daughter, and my brother and I were very protective of her. We took care of her during the summers when we had off from school, and my mom worked. There is a joke in my family that she never touched the ground for the first three years of her life because someone was always holding her or carrying her. She was our little princess. Her father (my stepdad) was a colder man, who did not show much emotion. There were times when he would light up looking at her though. He always kept all of us at arm's length and I think it had a lot to do with his daughter Katie, and her brain aneurysm.

Growing up, Ryann would always play dress up, but she was rarely a princess. She would pretend to be a ninja or something like that, and run around the house being "stealthy." She was not really a girly girl. She still isn't, other than the fact that she wears makeup and likes to shop. She played volleyball and Softball and was the captain of her team in both. She plays the violin and guitar and has a great singing voice. I wish I had half the talent she has. I always had to work really hard to get any skill in anything, and most things came naturally to her.

I left for the Air Force when Ryann was 6. I remember the night before I left I sat on her bed before she was about to fall asleep and told her that I had to go, I loved her and would miss her and would write her letters. She said she would write me letters, and she did. Her letters were always my favorite because they made me laugh. My mom would send me pictures of her when I was away, but it wasn't the same as actually getting to see her grow up. To me, she went from 6 to a teenager, and I missed her childhood because I was away. When I got home, I could barely recognize her, but my little ninja sister was still in there somewhere.

Ryann is very much like me in the fact that she is stubborn, and when she sets her mind to something she is going to get it. She is smart like me and can pass school with minimal outside effort. She also has some of the same anxieties as me, and sometimes seems depressed. That could just be because she is a teenage girl. My role in her life is to be a positive influence. A strong male role model for her since her father moved to North Carolina. I feel like I failed at this because of where my life was headed. She has even said to my mom before that she doesn't want to be 30 and living with her (which circumstances had led me to do). I decided to use my negative experiences to guide her in the right direction. I would often say that I am so skilled at failing, I can tell you exactly how not to do it. I see her making some of the same mistakes I made when I was younger, and I am trying to get her to move in a different direction. Again, she is stubborn, but so am I. I am persistent and patient and will keep trying to push her out of harm's way, so she can make a better life than I made. That is what you do for people you love. You do whatever you can to protect them.

Erin is my step-sister, but again I called her my sister. I met Erin when she was 4 years old, so I have known her for most of her life. When we were younger, she was the one that would get picked on by Nick and Katie. I tried to be nice to her, because she was the youngest out of us all and, to be honest, was accident-prone. She would often fall and get hurt. She was an adorable girl, and as she got older, she became fearless. I remember one time we went to Seabreeze, the local amusement park, and we went on this roller coaster that not only went up and down, and spun you upside down, but the seats themselves would rotate. There we are, getting thrashed around by this roller coaster, me screaming, and her as calm as a lake on a windless summer day, no expression to her face. No fear, but also no fun. I am not sure if she was masking her emotions, or her response to stress was just to shut down like mine has been.

Erin's relationship with her father, who is also Ryann's father, could be called rocky at best. Even now it has been many years since she has spoken to him. I often feel sorry for Erin because she had to grow up in a tough circumstance. At a young age her sister Katie would have her brain aneurysm only a day before her birthday. Erin spent her birthday in the hospital wondering if she would ever see her sister again. She was still young and did not fully understand what was going on. Her birthday is a constant reminder of what happened to her sister. That is just one day though. Katie required constant care, which meant Erin would always be placed second. This must have been hard for her growing up, but I believe she came out of the situation an incredibly strong woman. She is so smart and has a very bright future. A couple years ago she got married to a man named Simon. It looks like they are happy. After my mom and her dad got divorced, it was hard to keep in touch. She went to school 6 hours away, and both our lives are busy. I feel bad because I should be a better brother to her and talk to her more. For a couple years any time she came home from school, we would meet up at Tim Horton's and talk for about an hour to catch up. I wanted to make sure she was doing ok and would ask about Katie. I should have gone to see Katie, but I would always make excuses as to why I couldn't. It has been a while since I have seen Erin, and I believe she stopped telling me when she was going to be home. I understand though. She has a husband, and her own life, but I do think about her from time to time and hope she is okay.

Despite the many challenges Erin faced growing up she turned out to be really smart and driven. She completed college and is someone I would go to for advice on anything related to education, even though she is younger than me. She is lucky in that she has a loving family with her mother, and stepfather. No matter how far away she is or how little we speak to each other now, I hope she knows how proud I am of her.

Katie was the popular cheerleader in school. She had a lot of friends and was also very talented. I am not here to tell her story, not yet at least, but someone should because she has an incredible story, and she inspires people every day. We were the same age so growing up we hung out a lot. I would always look forward to her father getting visitation because that meant she would come over, and we could all play. The four of us would go get lost in the woods or camp out in the backyard, or go swimming, or play basketball. We were always doing something. We were in 8th grade when her aneurysm happened. A few weeks prior we had gone to the mall with my friends. I guess I ignored her because I was talking to some girl, and she became upset. We didn't fight often, but we did after that. Christmas was coming up, and we were shopping for presents. Don't ask me what I could afford in 8th grade because I have no idea. I think my mom gave me money and set us loose in the mall. I must have made her pretty upset because she did not talk to me for the rest of the day. Then when Christmas had arrived, she gave me a fake bag of coal for being an evil brother. I was stubborn and didn't want to hear it, so I pretty much ignored her that day. That would be the last day I would see her as a normal girl. The last day I would ever hear her speak or see her walk. The last day I saw her smile.

January 2nd, 2001, I was getting ready for school. It was our first day back after our long winter break. The phone rang. Ringing this early was strange. Katie's father was at the gym, and my mom was still sleeping. I answered the phone, and it was Katie and Erin's stepdad. He said something had happened and he needed to talk to my stepfather. I told him he wasn't home, so he asked for my mom. I woke up my mom and handed her the phone. She talked to him for a moment and then started to cry. I asked her what was going on, but she wouldn't tell me. I asked her if I should still go to school and she said yes. It wasn't long after that my grandfather showed up to my school to pick me up and bring me to the hospital where Katie was for surgery. An aneurysm burst to cause a brain bleed. She had 7 mini strokes, so they had to perform brain surgery to save her life. She had gone into a coma. I asked what happened and was told Katie was getting ready for school like she did every morning and she suddenly passed out. She wasn't breathing and had actually died for a short period of time. The EMT was able to resuscitate her on the way to the hospital. Katie always got terrible headaches, and the Doctor said they were warning signs. There is not much you can do to prevent this sort of thing from happening though, and it is pretty scary to think you could be getting ready in the morning one second, and the next you could be passed out on the floor.

We spent a lot of time at that hospital over the next few months. Katie was in a coma, and we were just waiting for a miracle. This event was the first time I ever saw her father cry. He would cry a lot and was scared to lose his daughter. I was afraid to lose my sister. The choice had been made to take her off of life support because the doctors told us that there was not a good chance of her coming out of this. My mom told me the night before they planned to do it, and I remember crying in my room because it wasn't fair that I had to lose my sister. The chapel at the church had sent a man named Simon to us who would pray with us and try to explain Gods plan for us all. He was doing his best to help us grieve through this process. He was a sincere man and truly did help us all. The day they had planned to turn off life support, Simon visited Katie. He held her hand and prayed. He then said, "Katie, if you are in there, please open your eyes." Katie opened her eyes, and Simon stood in shock. He immediately called in the Doctor and her father to tell them what had happened.

Katie was awake but paralyzed. She could not move. She could blink and had some communication skills. If we asked her questions, she would blink once for yes and twice for no. We had to stick to all yes and no questions. Now the doctors told us that she would probably never move again and would remain paralyzed. Soon after that Katie began to move her fingers. It wasn't much, but it was a start. Katie would spend the next couple months proving the doctors wrong at every turn. She was indeed a miracle (or this shows we really don't understand much about the brain and its function to heal itself). They sent her to a different location for rehab. They would teach her how to move again and a better way to communicate. It wasn't long before she was able to sit up. They got her a motorized wheelchair so she could move around. She still could not breathe on her own, but she was getting better. It is true that she will never be the same, and she has lost all feeling and movement to one side of her face. She can't talk, but she does know sign language now and lives a pretty good life at home. She has the care she needs and seems happy.

All of this cost a lot of money, so we held fundraisers. Some of Katie's friends made purple ribbons, and people would buy them and wear them to support her. I always wore mine to school. Many of the kids in school didn't know what happened, and I was shy, so I didn't talk about it. I would get picked on for wearing a purple ribbon, and people would call me gay or other names. I did not care. I wore it for her, and if she could go through everything she did to survive against all the odds, I could take a little harassment.

I have a large Italian family, with over 20 cousins. Family get-togethers growing up were always my favorite because I would get to see everyone, and we always had a great time. Now all my cousins are adults and have families of their own, so it makes it hard to get together. I see them around the holidays, and we have a family reunion every July. My siblings and my family meant a lot to me. I would tell myself that this is the reason I did what I had to do to keep everyone safe. To protect them from any attacks. To protect them from losing me. These people are my "why" to the "what" I have done.

I was the firstborn child, so you can call me the learning curb. My parents did the best they could, and I love them for what they have given me. However, depression runs in my genes. My father was severely depressed when I was growing up, and I did not know it at the time. It wasn't until recently that I understood how he felt when I was younger, and I could pick up on the signs and symptoms of depression. There were days when he would sleep a lot or not talk much. Sometimes he was on a short fuse and would get angry over small things and take it out on my brother and me. We didn't care. In fact, when we were younger, we preferred his company over my mom's. Most of the time he was a really awesome father. He would take us places, like the park or to movies and sporting events. He would rent movies for a Friday night, or make delicious snack foods to eat while watching stand-up comedy. He would also play video games with us. To me, he was the best father I could ask for.

One day my view of my father would change. It was the summer of my junior year in High School, and my dad was not answering my phone calls. It had been a couple days since I had seen him, and the fourth of July had passed, and he usually went with my brother and me to see fireworks. We began to worry. My uncle had a spare key to his apartment, so I called him and met him and my aunt over at his residence.

"Hey, Matthew," My aunt said as she rubbed my back trying to comfort me. I could tell she was as concerned as I was. My uncle greeted me, and then we all headed for my father's door. I will never forget the way his apartment looked as the door swung open. His lights were on, and there was food on the stove and dishes in the sink. The apartment was a mess, which was uncommon for my father. It looked as if he left in a hurry. My uncle's face went from his usual smile to a look of concern.

"Jerry!" He yelled out. No answer. "Well let's look around."

We began to search the apartment. I took the living room; my uncle went to the kitchen, and my aunt went to his bedroom. Only a minute went by before I heard my aunt sobbing from my father's room. She was trying to stay quiet, so I wouldn't hear her. She called to my uncle, and he went into the room with her.

They both walked out of the room, my aunt holding a piece of paper in her hands. I was sitting on the floor, or maybe I dropped to the floor after she walked out with the paper. She fell down and hugged me.

"What's it say?" I said with tears streaming down my face. She held me tighter.

"What's it say?" I repeated. Still, no response.

"What's it say? What's it say? What's it say?" I repeated over and over again, now becoming hysterical. She never answered me, but I thought the worse.

"We don't know where he is or what happened so let's stay calm and figure this out." My uncle said, trying to stay strong for the both of us. "Let's take Matt home."

My aunt nodded in agreement. She drove my car, while my uncle drove me home in his. They did not want me to drive in the state I was in. We pulled up in the driveway, and I walked inside with my aunt and uncle who explained everything to my mom. My brother was not at home yet and did not know what was going on. My mom asked me to keep it a secret from him. So, I did.

A few more days went by and still no sign of my father. I have no idea what my aunt and uncle did after they dropped me off, and we never talked about that day again. Finally, my father returned home or was brought back. I am unsure how the events unfolded as to how he came to be at his apartment, but at the time I did not care. I was just happy he was alright. I went over to his house to see him, and he was lying in his bed. I sat beside him, and he just gave me a big hug and whispered "I'm sorry" to me. After that I said nothing. He said nothing. We never talked about it again. It was that day that I realized how much my dad was hurting.

My Mother isn't without her problems. I am grateful for everything she has done for me, but she too is on medication for anxiety. She is in her 50s, but you would never guess based on the way she looks. She looks younger than most 30-year old's. She is active at the gym, goes on vacation 2 to 3 times a year, lives in a huge house, with a beautiful yard, and makes great money working for herself from home. Despite this, her depression and anxiety still get the best of her at times, and she has not learned the right coping skills to deal with it positively. Something I hope to help her with one day. Her parents (my grandparents) were the most amazing people and raised her right. They were even there all the time for my brother and me growing up. I swear we saw them more than our actual parents, and for that, I am incredibly thankful because they were the greatest.

With my parents both having their own mental disorders, I often wonder if it provided a blank canvas, ready for my mind to create its own diseases. A new work of art inspired by the genetic makeup of those who created me. Was I doomed from the start? Was I fated for this life from birth? What about my brother and sister? Maybe they are more like me than I realize because we never talk about it. I often think about these questions and hope that they don't turn out like me. I try my hardest to guide them away from my path, but they both follow so closely.

Here is why college never made sense to me. You pay for an education to get a job that you will probably hate to pay back the loan you took out to get the job in the first place. Then you work hard for 40 years and retire for 20 and "enjoy" your golden years. This never seemed like a good plan for me. I understand that not everyone can be a Business owner, and the world needs janitors and garbage men, and Doctors and factory workers to keep moving. That is why we are taught that the "right thing" to do is to go to college, get an education, get a job, get married, have kids, retire, and die. This will keep an economy going, and a country going if everyone conformed to this cycle. This was not for me. I think I get my entrepreneurial spirit from my Grandfather and my Mother who both owned their own businesses. I did not yet have the skills or the capital (or a good idea for that matter) to open up my own business, so I needed a plan.

This is where I really started to crave success. The Air Force would mold me into someone who always wanted more. I was always looking for that next rank, that next promotion, the next big deal, and was never satisfied where I was. It was the start of my poisonous ambition. The need for more would always be what led me to lose what I have and end up with less. Such an unfortunate irony that would assist in guiding me down a path of madness. It all stems from this one choice, and conversations with friends and family that provided great hope that my future would be bright, in a time when I was still innocent at heart.

The two most significant transitions in my life were entering the Air Force and leaving it. August 1st, 2006 at 0400 and my alarm went off, though it was not needed. I had not slept. I was laying there in my hotel bed in downtown Buffalo NY thinking about what I was about to do. I remember my roommate was also having trouble, as he seemed to sleep talk and walk; something that might be an issue for him later on down the road. That was none of my concern though. I laid there for about ten minutes after my alarm went off before I decided to get up, grab my stuff and head down to the breakfast buffet that the hotel had prepared for us. I ate a pretty good meal and then jumped on the bus to MEPS (Military Entrance Processing Station) to out-process. This is where they look at you one last time to make sure nothing has changed, and you are still qualified to join the military. By 1300 we were off to the Airport.

I had never been on a plane before, so this had me a little nervous. Someone who had just joined the Air Force has never been on a Plane before. Ironic, I know. I got lucky though. Sitting next to me on my first flight ever was an older gentleman who reminded me a lot of my grandfather, who I had seen as my best friend, my mentor, and the person who did the majority of raising me. This man talked like him and struck up a conversation with me. I think he could tell I was nervous.

"So, where are you headed, son?" The elderly man asked

"San Antonio, Sir. I am going to Basic Training."

"Ahh, well thank you for your service. Have you ever been on a plane before?"

"No Sir."

"It's not so bad. I have flown hundreds of times. First, we will taxi out to the runway, and get up to speed to take off. Do you like roller coasters?"

"Yes," I answered, even though at the time I was not a huge fan of roller coasters either.

"Good. It feels like that at first. Once we take off, you will hear a loud bang. That's just the landing gear folding up into the plane, so don't be worried."

"Okay"

"Once we get up in the Air, it's smooth sailing from there. A couple of times we might hit some turbulence, and the plane will rock, but don't worry, these pilots know what they are doing."

After he explained what would happen, he changed the subject to talk about my hobbies, and we exchanged stories. I think this was to take my mind off flying, and the daunting task I was about to undergo. The sad thing is I don't even know his name and would never see him again. I am not sure if he is even still alive.

I learned that my fear, much like all fears, was based on the unknown. I did not know what to expect when flying, or what would happen when I got to San Antonio. When you take the unknown out of the equation, the fear turns into anticipation. You can mentally prepare for the trials to come, and you are more likely to get through it. I appreciate what that old man did for me that day.

Finally, I had arrived at the San Antonio International Airport. It was very late, about 0100 in the morning. I think they did that on purpose. Everything they did seemed to be a way to drain us mentally or break us down. I followed the crowd of other "kids" to a spot where we all looked to be meeting up. I remember my recruiter telling me not to sit on the furniture when I got there because they would target us. We have not earned the right to sit on chairs yet. I sat on the floor. A man in a uniform and an intimidating looking hat walked in and started yelling. He formed us up and told us to march down the hall and outside to the buses. We all got on and had our IDs checked. The Military Training Instructor (MTI) then got off the bus, and we started driving to Lackland Air Force Base. On our way there, the Bus driver came over the loudspeaker.

"Good evening everyone. I am sure a lot of you are in shock right now and scared about what is going to happen next. First, I want to say I am very proud of each and every one of you. When you get off the bus, the MTI's will yell at you and be mean. It's their job. It's nothing against you so don't take it personally. After about two weeks they will start to lighten up, and you will see them more as a father figure. Remember, they want you to pass and succeed. You are part of their family now. Good luck out there."

This made me feel good. It made me feel like I belonged there. This feeling lasted for about another 3 minutes until we pulled up to in-process. An MTI then came on the bus and screamed at us to get off. We all exited the bus and formed up on the pad. All of us had our bags, and they told us to put them down. This is where the mind games began. At the time we didn't know why they did it, but now I understand. They wanted us to move as one. We didn't put them down all at the same time, so they yelled at us to pick them up. We were ordered to say, "preceding sir" whenever they told us to do something. Again, we failed to do this as a unit, so they told us to put them down. "Preceding sir" Pick them up. "Preceding sir" Put them down "preceding sir." This went on for what seemed like an hour until we all were doing it at the exact same time. They started to call us inside one by one to in-process. They gave us food, which later we came to call "boxed nasties." It was a frozen sandwich, with an ice block that was supposed to be a Capri Sun. I did not really get to eat or drink anything. I didn't mind. I was under a lot of stress and wasn't hungry anyway. Plus, it was about 2am at this point. Once we all in-processed we were separated into flights and sent off to our Dorms. They rushed us in, had us strip down and shower.

I can honestly say there is only one thing that I was mad at my recruiter for. He did not check to make sure I had shower shoes. He did not even tell me about shower shoes. I had to shower in my actual shoes. My sneakers. My black sneakers. They got soaked, and I would need to spend the next three days walking around in them in the middle of July, in San Antonio Texas. I was miserable. The showers were a bay style with six shower heads. We had to go in there with soap in our hands and count to 3 for each shower head. When you had moved through each one, you were done, so if you are good at Math, then you know that every day we took 18-second showers. Only enough time to wash what was important. Then we were rushed through shaving. Even if people didn't have any facial hair, they were forced to shave. I have never seen so many people bleed in my life as I did that first night. People left the latrine with blood and shaving cream still on their faces. There were 52 of us, and we were all showered and shaved in under 10 minutes. We then all sat in the Dayroom to get debriefed. It was now close to 0400. There were two bays in our dorm. I stayed in A-Bay.

Once we were done getting screamed at for the night, we all got into our bunks, and they shut off the lights. The MTI's left, and there was silence. Silence, only for a couple of minutes. I believe everyone was in shock. People did not know what to do or say. Then the tears started. I had never heard so many grown men cry as I did that night. I did not cry though. I had been yelled at before, so it did not really bother me. Being away from home didn't bother me either. The worst part of that night to me was getting my shoes wet.

Whenever a new flight comes in, they send newly graduated Airman in 7th week to patrol the dorm at night. This is called Dorm guard. They would do it for the first three nights until we learned how. The Dorm guards were pretty cool though. They calmed us all down and told us what we could expect because they had just gone through all of it. Most of the advice they give was cliché, and you probably had heard it in an advertisement or some propaganda before. Such classics as "It doesn't get easier, but you get better" or "You need to learn to follow before you can lead." At the time though it was pretty comforting.

By the time we went to sleep it was 5am, so they told us that we were going to sleep in a little bit because we were up so late. Sleeping in at this place was sleeping until 0700 since we usually would wake up at 4am. 7am hit, and we heard the sounds of revelry. For those of you who have never heard revelry before, it is the worst version of your alarm clock you could ever imagine. I urge you to look it up. Then imagine waking up to that every morning for 7 weeks, accompanied by the screams of your MTI. Revelry went off, and our MTI was in and screaming and throwing bunks and telling us to get ready faster. It didn't matter how quickly we could get prepared, it would never be fast enough.

My MTI's were Staff Sergeant Corrilo and Staff Sergeant Antuna. You never forget your MTI. Corrilo was a middle-sized man who had a sort of thug persona to him. At the time we were terrified of him. Antuna was new to the world of being an MTI, so he was not yet as ruthless or mean when it came to us. He would sometimes yell, but for the most part, you could call him the "good cop" out of the two. He was short and skinny, but you still didn't want to make him mad. The power the MTI's had over us was more than just physical. They could make a good day bad, and a bad day worse. They controlled where you went, what you were doing at all times, when you could eat when you could sleep, and when you could breathe. You did nothing without their permission. It took great mental fortitude and the will to complete this training to make it through. Some people weren't cut out for it.

I remember an Airman we would call Mmbop. He was having a hard time in Basic and wanted to leave. He was a smaller kid, with red hair and glasses. The kind of kid you knew was picked on his whole life and had something to prove, so he joined the military. He probably never had many friends, but now he had us. We had this fat kid get recycled into our flight because he was a failure. His goal was to get kicked out because he no longer wanted to be in the Air Force. I walked into the latrine one day to see this fat kid talking to Mmbop.

"It's easy. All you have to do is make them think you are crazy. Pretend you want to hurt yourself." The fat kid said to Mmbop.

"What the hell is going on in here?" I asked.

"Mmbop wants out, and I am helping him," Said the fat washout.

"No, you're not. Mmbop, you aren't going anywhere. Come to talk to me and don't listen to this fat piece of crap." I took Him by the arm and led him back to his bunk.

"Hey. What's going on?" I asked.

"I don't know. I just want to go home. I can't do this for four years."

"Dude. It isn't going to be like this for four years. This is all a mental game they are playing with us. In a few weeks, we will be out of here, and it will get better. You will see."

"You think so?"

"Yes. Come on. Your recruiter didn't tell you about this? The mental games, and then how real Air Force life is? Do you really want to be like that fat loser in there? You are better than that. We will help you through. Okay?"

"Yes, sir. Thank you."

Airman Mmbop did end up graduating with us, and the fat kid did end up getting kicked out. I saw a few people get kicked out in boot camp and I often wondered what life was like for them. To the people that got kicked out of Basic training, this was traumatic. It was so bad that they could not do it anymore, so they were sent home. I wonder if anyone ever got PTSD from basic training. Did they have nightmares to remind them of what they went through in basic? To me, this seems silly, but it's all relative. To some, my encounter and flashbacks may be silly. To Marines, and Combat Airman that has been in large-scale battles and have killed more, my event might seem like nothing. As meaningless as those that found Basic Training too challenging to complete.

When people think of Military Basic Training, I am sure an image goes through their head. The ones that have never been picture shooting ranges and patrolling through a forest or mud. Obstacle courses, and constant physical training (PT). Well, that is not really what it is like. Sure, there are times when we do those things, but a lot of basic training is sitting in class and learning. You learn about customs and courtesies, history, proper wear of uniform, regulations, and the Uniform Code of Military Justice, which governs us all. You are tested on all this knowledge and need to pass before you can graduate from BMT.

"I am a 320th trainee. I am a highly motivated, truly dedicated, aim high never die Air Force recruit." We would recite this multiple times a day. So much so, that even now, 13 years later, I can remember it so vividly. I don't want to say they brainwashed us, but most of what they did you could see to be some form of brainwashing. Either the chants and sayings we would recite, or the videos of bombs dropping on the enemy set to the soundtrack of "let the bodies hit the floor." They said it was for moral, but looking back at it now, it seemed like they were brainwashing us to feel invincible. They would have to. If we didn't feel that way, why would we willingly put ourselves in harm's way and do what needed to be done? Later in my career, I would learn how none of us are invincible and find out firsthand the consequences of our actions. We were called the Gators. "Roll gator roll" was our slogan, and that's what we did. No matter what the world threw at us, we just kept rolling.

The bomb run was where we would march past the command for review. It was our graduation. Every flight graduating would form up and march past friends, family, and the command so they could see what we had accomplished. Every Airman, every Air Force hero and legend had marched the bomb run, so it was an honor to be among the ranks of heroes. We were picked for flag mass. This meant that we would carry our Nations colors; all of them. Every state flag. I got Oregon. We were different. We would draw extra attention, so we needed to be perfect. The week prior we spent 4 or 5 hours a day practicing for the bomb run to make sure we had it perfect. We executed it without any problems, and I got to see my family for the first time in 8 weeks right after that.

My Mother and Step Father at the time came to see me, and my girlfriend who I was still with from high school. We got to go to the River Walk in downtown San Antonio. It was nice to get off base and see normal life again. I got to eat a steak in a nice restaurant and go into a lot of the local shops. We had to be careful of what we did or how we behaved though. We were still in uniform, and they had MTIs walking around in civilian clothes to try to catch us breaking any rules, such as drinking or smoking or using things we weren't supposed to have yet. If you were caught, they would "recycle" you back to week 1, and you would be forced to go through basic training all over again. This happened to a few people, but no one in my flight. I wasn't dumb enough to risk another 8 weeks of my life. Also, I was not old enough to drink, and never smoked anything before, so I really didn't have any temptations or desire to.

As Graduation weekend came to a close, I said goodbye to my family and prepared to leave the next morning for Wichita Falls, Texas. This is where I would go for Tech School, to learn how to do my job as a weapon specialist. I remember the night before we left we were allowed to have all of our stuff back. I had brought my PSP, a portable gaming system and some movies that would play on it. I watched "Resident Evil: Nemesis" that night. We had to get up early to out-process, but all of us were so excited that we graduated, we did not sleep much.

I remember thinking that the hard times were over. No more getting yelled at, no more prison type lifestyle, no more involuntary push-ups. Life was about to get good. Boy, was I wrong. The Air Force was smart about how they did things. If you cage a dog for an extended amount of time and then just open the cage, the dog will go wild. If you move the dog from a cage to a short leash, and then a slightly longer leash, the dog cannot go wild. The same principle applied to us. We were caged dogs. They could not give us back all our freedoms at once. We would not know what to do with them all, and most likely people would get in trouble, so the Air Force had a phase system. We would slowly get some freedoms back over the next couple months to ensure a safe transition back into "normal" life.

Basic training taught me a couple lessons. The first one was how much I appreciated all my freedoms. It's true that you don't know what you have until it's gone. They took away all our liberties, and we were now prisoners of the United States Air Force. The second thing I learned was how much I really appreciated my parents, my friends, my family, and all the things they have done for me over the years. I wrote a letter home to my mom telling her I was sorry for every time I didn't listen to her and for not appreciating her more when I was home.

There is so much more I could talk about how my brain was developed to be the perfect candidate for a mental disorder, but it would be irrelevant. What I am saying is we all have a past that writes the programming for how our minds think. What our morals are. What things will be seen as disturbing, and what things can seem reasonable. It is setting up a blank canvas and providing the different colors of paint to begin work on our mental masterpiece. Mine came out titled "PTSD," but given another background, a different childhood, it might have come out differently. Before I even went to Afghanistan, the stage was set for what could and would happen to me. It just needed to play out.

Chapter 3

FEEDING THE DEMON

"Welcome to Afghanistan." Those words played over and over in my head as I remember landing and de-boarding the C-17 when we first arrived. These words were spoken by the current base commander who came to greet us as we first laid eyes on the mountain view from the flight line. "Welcome to Afghanistan," he said with a handshake. As if we were there for a friendly visit, or even had a choice to go to that part of the world. At the time, I did not care. I was excited to be there. Excited to be a part of "Operation Enduring Freedom." The name of the campaign in Afghanistan at first confused me. The "Enduring" part, as if freedom was something that needed to be endured. You endure hardships, like losing a life, or having your house burned down, but freedom should not be something that needs to be endured. That was how I thought when I first arrived. That is how Americans grow up thinking, no matter how many times you hear the term "freedom isn't free." You never truly understand the meaning of that statement. In this place having freedom means you are a target. Supporting the United States efforts in Afghanistan made you a target. If you wanted to be free in this country, it meant that there were people who wanted you dead, so freedom needed to be endured.

It is something you might talk about in school or in principle. Is freedom worth dying for? For many of the Afghani natives it was. Many were tired of living in fear of religious persecution and wanted to be able to think for themselves. This caused a lot of them to support us while we were there. Or did it? Maybe these people were just conditioned to please the people holding the guns. I often wonder what they really thought about us. We showed up and basically said, "Be free or else."

After that fateful night, I let my thoughts run wild. The majority of the days we had left in this place I would let my mind get the best of me. I was once a carefree boy, but now I was a soulless man. How could I go home to face my family, or my soon to be daughter? What kind of father would I be now? Would she grow up to be a better person without me? I did not think I was going to make it back to the states, and I was ok with that. I could no longer picture a future for my life. I was experiencing absolute loneliness.

"Hey, Alto, are you ok?" Airman Padgett said to me as I stared into nothingness.

"Yeah man, I'm fine," I answered.

"Ok, because you seem kind of out of it."

"I just didn't sleep well."

"OK. I wonder what today has in store for us."

"Probably nothing. Load some jets, play some games, and wait for the sun to rise."

"True."

To be honest, that is what the majority of our days held for us in Afghanistan. There are a lot of war movies out there with exciting battles, and a ton of action scenes, but the film I found to be most accurate to what war is really like is Jarhead. It tells how boring war can be and how most of the time you are just sitting around waiting for something to happen. Most of the time we spent playing cards or guitar hero on the Xbox that a Tech Sergeant brought, while we waited for our 12-hour shift to end. Our shift was 1800 to 0600, so we saw the sun set and rise on our shift. Most of our work was done in the dark, with only a headlamp to see, so we didn't give away our position to the enemy, who might try to aim rockets in at us if we used a light-all. I wonder what effect the constant darkness had on my mental state after the event.

Before the incident that night, I would enjoy most of our downtime with my crew. Padgett was my age, a little taller, and a great guy. He was like a brother to me when we were deployed. Staff Sergeant Garcia was our crew lead, and she took care of us. She wasn't perfect, but I learned a lot from her, including what kind of Staff Sergeant I wanted to be one day. She would take out the trash and do the low-level jobs because she would say she isn't above doing the labor, and if her troops had to do it then she would too. That is where I adopted my "I won't ever ask an Airman to do something I didn't do" mentality. Some of the other Sergeants would use their power to get out of work and make their Airman do it, but never mine. We always did everything as a crew, which is why I believe we were so good. I kept track of every bomb and bullet I ever loaded in Afghanistan, and we usually loaded the most out of any crew. Our munitions always worked, and the mission always got done. I was proud of the things I had done in Afghanistan, including taking out Osama Bin Laden's number 2 guy the first week we were there.

After the event took place, however, I found little joy in anything we did. Most of the time I would sit out on a bench and stare off into the mountains. I would look up at the stars and wonder if there was more to life than all this. I would wait for the sun to rise because it meant it was almost time for my shift to end, and then I could go back to my bunk and try to sleep. I found that I was always tired now but was hardly able to sleep. Most nights I would let my mind run loose and imagine a thousand different ways to die. I would look up more videos of people dying and then put myself in that situation. The most unnerving feeling in the world is to realize you are going to die and honestly know what that means. Everyone knows they are going to die, so that is not what I am talking about. To watch someone die, and really understand what that means is something completely different. To hear them take their last breath, and watch the light leave their eyes. To see the fear on their face as they approach the unknown. To know that one day, that will be you. You never know when, or how it is going to happen, but you know that one day that will be your fear, your last breath, and the light leaving your eyes.

They say time heals all, but in reality, it ends all things. There is no way to escape the inevitable realization that one day you will die. I don't believe this is where the fear comes from though. At least not for me. It comes from not being smart enough to make a real difference in the world but being just smart enough to realize my shortcomings. These are the thoughts that feed the demon and make him grow. The ones who created the monster I was becoming, who would terrorize the ones I once cared for when I returned to the United States. My demon was anger, rage, fear, and self-doubt. He grew stronger each day as I awaited my return to the "real world." A lot had happened on that deployment, and perhaps one day I will talk about it, but that day is not today. The cause of the birth of my demon has been established, so now it is time to introduce him to the United States and my family.

The night before we left Afghanistan to come home I was standing outside the USO on base. I looked up at the sky one last time and wondered if I would ever see this place again. Would I ever gaze upon the beautiful mountains of Afghanistan and see the sunrise from behind them? The view of peace in a time of chaos. It was the only thing that kept me going. Some would call it hope. Would I ever see the sun rise over the mountain again?

On my way home, a single conversation had entered my mind. It is the one I had with my wife, Alyssa before I left. The night before I left, I was feeling scared. My wife was pregnant, and I would miss the whole pregnancy.

"When you get back, we should move off base and get a bigger place, so we have room for the baby."

"I'm not coming back," I replied abruptly. She began to cry.

"Don't you think I know that?" She said.

I looked at her, rolled over and went to sleep.

"I'm not coming back." I suppose that much was true because I didn't. At the time I thought I was going to die over there, but something worse happened. The Matt that left Arizona for Afghanistan was gone. He would never come back. Who was he? He was kind to everyone, hated conflict, and wanted to live a happy life and impress the people who cared about him. He tried to take care of his family, and country, and do something with his life. R.I.P Matt, who was no more in 2007. In his place was a mentally abusive, sociopath who hated himself so much, he wanted others to hate him as well. How would he accomplish this? By first making them love him, trust him, and need him. Then he would rip it all away. I never did this on purpose, but it was always how it played out, and each time it did I lost a little more of myself. I thought I would never get it back.

I landed back in Tucson Arizona, at Davis-Monthan AFB on October 23rd, 2007. We got off the plane and were met by base leadership, who greeted us with "Welcome Home" and a handshake. Behind them, in one of the hangers were the friends and families of everyone on the deployment, including my extremely pregnant wife. She was due any day now. She stood with my friend Madrid's wife. I hardly recognized her. She looked so different from how I remembered, and my memory seemed to have been altered. In fact, when I would remember my life before Afghanistan, it is almost as if I am watching someone else's memories. I do not recognize that person or any of the people he knew. It was as if I was seeing Alyssa for the first time, only this version of myself did not like her. I walked up to her and gave her a hug anyway. After all, she was carrying my daughter. We went home, and I decided to shower and take a nap. I needed it after the long trip I had just come from. I was now a cold-hearted man and would not be overly affectionate.

The next morning, I needed to check in with my shop and in-process before starting my R&R. My flight chief was there and wanted to speak with me.

"Airman Altobelli. May I speak to you for a moment?"

"Yes Sir, what can I do for you?"

"Your baby is due any day now right?" He asked

"That's right."

"How would you like to transfer to the 58th? That way you won't have to deploy again for some time and can spend some time with your family."

The 358th was nicknamed the Lobos, and it was a training squadron. I was currently a part of the 354th (Bulldogs) which was the only deployable A-10 squadron on base. I was shocked that he gave me the opportunity to switch to a different squadron, and part of me thinks he was filled in on what had happened to me and that is why he wanted me to have a lot of time away from the war. Other people had small children or babies, but he asked me. I am not sure if that is the reason, and I did not ask too many questions. I accepted his offer and transferred to the Lobos. I would miss my old crew, but I knew they would understand.

I do believe that a few people in my leadership were informed about what happened that night in Afghanistan because I was required to check in with mental health on base and would have to go a few times before being cleared to go back to work. I did not really like the psychiatrist they had on base. He was an older man who had no emotion on his face. He would ask me the routine questions like did I think about hurting myself, or anyone else. I just told him what he wanted to hear. I went and saw him three times before he cleared me and said I no longer needed to come in. I should have been more honest, but he wasn't really great at his job and didn't make me feel like opening up. I guess the Air Force needed to make sure they checked all their boxes in case I went crazy they could say they "did all they could."

I would enjoy the next month off from work as I used some leave after my R&R since I was going to be a new father and wanted to get used to the role. October 31st, 2007 came around, and my daughter was born. I remember the first time I saw her I thought she was the most beautiful baby I had ever seen. I was the first one to hold her after they cleaned her up. They handed her to me, and she stopped crying. I sat in the chair next to Alyssa's bed with my baby daughter, Morgan, swaddled up in my arms. Her eyes were open, and it looked like she was staring right at me, or perhaps through me. I know they say babies can't see when they are born but it really felt like she saw me. Her timing was perfect. She was the Angel to fight back my Demon. At this moment I no longer felt lost. I knew I loved this little girl and needed to do anything I could to protect her. She had reminded me what love was. A little bit of myself was born again with her, and that is the piece that keeps fighting back the evil that lives inside of me.

Shortly after Morgan was born, I called my dad.

"Hey, Matt" He answered.

"Hi Dad, she's here!"

"Awesome. Congratulations buddy. How does she look?"

"She is the most beautiful baby I have ever seen."

We talked for a minute, but I needed to call everyone else, so I hung up with him and made the rounds. Once I was done, I went into dad mode. Alyssa was still out of it from giving birth, so I needed to take care of Morgan. I would feed her and burp her and change her. One thing they don't warn you about is the tar-like substance that babies poop out right after they are born. It is super sticky and hard to wipe off. I asked the nurse about it, and she said it was normal. After a few days of being in the hospital, we were ready to go home. Alyssa's Dad was flying down to Tucson to stay with us for a few days and help out since we were moving. We decided to get a larger apartment off base and bank some extra money now that we had a new addition to the family. I had to go to the Airport to pick him up.

I pulled up to the Airport and helped him load his luggage into the car. The drive back to the apartment was pretty quiet. He was usually a calm man, and I was too. He only asked me a few questions.

"What was it like over there?"

"Different" I answered

"Did you see some pretty messed up stuff?"

"Yeah"

At that point, he stopped talking. Maybe he figured I didn't want to talk about it. Making me think about it brought me back down to reality. It was as if the demon had cracked open a window and whispered, "I'm still here. We will play later." I tried to get it out of my head and only focus on the good things going on right now, like my baby daughter. If I was going to raise her right I had no room for this other side of me to be peeking through.

The New apartment was small, but adequate. Morgan had her own room, and we had ours. It's had two bathrooms, a good size kitchen, and family room. Alyssa's father was a huge help in setting things up and taking care of Morgan while we got everything just right. Then the time came to fly back to NY to see the rest of the family with our newborn. Looking back now, it might not have been a great idea to fly with a 2-week-old baby, but we did it anyway. She was actually terrific on the plane. She did not cry and slept pretty much the whole way to New York.

The trip itself was rather unremarkable. We visited with family, and they got to see Morgan. The only time I can remember from this trip home was a time in our local grocery store, Wegmans. My sister, Ryann's birthday was coming up, and I was standing in the card aisle. I was reading and must have blocked out the world around me. All of a sudden, I felt a tap on my hip as a lady rammed her cart into me and said: "MOVE!" The Cart only had Arizona Ice tea in it, but about 5 of them, which I found to be ironic due to where I had just come from, and the fact that I loved Arizona Iced Tea when I was in high school. I felt myself fill with rage and hate. This was an older lady who looked miserable. About a hundred thoughts flooded through my head all at once. Thoughts such as, "why are you so angry? You live in America. What can you possibly be mad about? Why do you need so much Arizona Ice tea?" I decided to pick up her cart and throw it, which scared her. I don't really remember what happened next, but I know I had to leave. This event had a specific significance to it. It was the beginning of my transformation after I got home into someone I did not want to be. The first time I could not control my anger. It would only get worse from here.

Back in Arizona, we were settling into our new life, and I had to go back to work. I began on day shift to go through qualifications with my new crew and get to know them. My new crew lead was Staff Sergeant Morris, and my 3 man was Airman Angley. Morris was a tall man who enjoyed his Belgium beers. Angley was also from New York, was my age, and very good at his job. It did not take long for our crew to click on a professional level. We were good at what we did and were often the go-to team for maintenance to be done on any weapons systems. We moved to swing shift which was 3pm to 11pm, but we would often have to stay past midnight to finish up big jobs. On this crew, I won more awards and got more recognition than I ever had before in my career. I have Staff Sergeant Morris to thank for that, but he would never let me get a big head about it and would often bring me back down to reality by knocking me down a peg. If I were taking too long on a job he would say "Come on maintenance professional of the year, why are you moving so slow?" Just to remind me that I was no better than anyone else out there, and I too had my bad days. This may make him sound like a jerk, but to be honest, he was probably the best supervisor I had ever had because of it. He always challenged me to do better.

My work life was great, but my personal life suffered. Morgan was a baby and having a new baby was hard on my relationship. Alyssa would want me to get up in the middle of the night with Morgan when she cried, and we would take turns. Some nights I was too tired from working all day and wouldn't even hear her cry so Alyssa would wake me up in an unpleasant fashion so I could go take care of Morgan. One night I let the anger get the best of me. I could not get Morgan to stop crying. I tried everything. I fed her, changed her, rocked her, but nothing. She was still screaming. I remember yelling at her to go back to bed. This obviously made no sense because she was just a baby and could not understand what I was saying, or even understand why she was crying. This was my demon breaking through and reminding me I was not fit to be a father. I put her back in her crib and held her down as she tried to move around and scream. In my mind, I thought if she weren't moving she would fall back asleep, but in reality, I was crazy and doing crazy things. Alyssa came out now and started yelling at me.

"What are you doing!?"

"I am trying to get her back to sleep. She won't stop crying."

"You're hurting her!"

"Shut up, both of you just shut up!"

I was unable to handle it and stormed in my room and slammed the door, leaving Morgan to Alyssa. I failed to be the father she needed at the time. I knew this, and it became increasingly recognizable to Alyssa. She hated living away from New York. Away from her friends and family. Away from any support. She would often pick huge fights with me so I would buy her a plane ticket home, so she could see everyone, and then eventually makeup with me and fly back. I usually only made up with her because I missed my daughter so much. It was obvious to me that I no longer had feelings for my wife.

We went on like this for a little over a year before Alyssa had enough of me and decided she would be leaving for good. I came home from work one night to her bags packed.

"What are you doing?" I asked

"We are leaving, Matt."

"Why? You can't take my daughter away from me."

"Yes, I can. There is nothing for me here, and I am not happy. Morgan is coming with me."

"Fine. When Does your flight leave?" I said, not putting up much of a fight.

"In the morning."

I was too proud to stop her from leaving, and honestly, I thought this was one of the times when she would be home for a couple weeks and then want to come back. (I wonder how much money I spent on plane tickets over the years.) That was not the case this time. Months went by, and she got a boyfriend. She was serious and moving on with her life. That was not the sad part though. What hurt me the most was walking by my daughter's room every day. I left it exactly how it was the day she left. There were even still some toys on the floor. I would look in there and become depressed. I would spend hours just sitting on her floor, visualizing her in her crib or playing with her toys. She was so far away from me, and there was nothing I could do. I did not want her to grow up not knowing who I was. Eventually, the pain became too much for me to bare, and I shut her door. This would also lock the last bit of humanity I had left in that room with her belongings. I would not look in there again until I was ready to clean it out. I was alone.

To say I was alone isn't really fair to my "friends" who came back with me from Afghanistan. I would see them occasionally, and they would drive me mad. Just looking at me, sometimes alive, sometimes dead. I would have dreams that I was back in Afghanistan. Sometimes it was a normal day, where nothing happened. Sometimes the dreams would be things that didn't happen but were as chaotic as that night. I would see them, and they looked at me like I was the reaper. They never spoke to me, but I would make them speak. If they could talk, what would they say? I would talk to myself often. I would walk into the bathroom sometimes and peer into the mirror at myself. I would get so close to the mirror that I could see the pores on my skin. I would say out loud "I hate you." I would scream it sometimes and break down either crying or laughing. My life seemed like one giant joke. Sometimes things went so bad it was actually comical. I didn't know things could be this bad, so it made it funny. I was really messed up.

My professional life had not suffered at all though. I was always able to separate my personal life from work, and really get in the zone when I was working. I even got promoted to Senior Airman 6 months early. One of only 2 people in the squadron to be given this honor. 8 months went by, and I was about to go on leave and visit my daughter. I was excited. Being without her for 8 months, my hope started to fade. The longer I went without her, the crazier I became. I would run scenarios through my head. Bad ones. Ones where I hurt myself or hurt others. I would spend a lot of time by myself, playing video games and trying to get lost in another world. I would always pick games that had a deep story with choices and consequences, like Mass Effect or Dragon Age. This allowed you to be a paragon or a renegade. Essentially good or bad. I always took the villain route, because secretly I always wanted to be the villain. It's easier, isn't it? To knowingly do wrong, but not worry about the consequences or others. It sounds great. My problem is that in real life I am the complete opposite. I do wrong on accident and care for all those I hurt. I feel their pain every day. I have met some great people and got very close to them, only to lose them in the end.

My crew had been working on a hard-broke jet for over a month, essentially rewiring the whole thing. Aircraft 651 (I will never forget those numbers). Angley was mad that I was leaving, and we weren't finished with it yet, but I needed to go and see my daughter.

"I can't believe you are leaving me to finish up this shit by myself," he said.

"Come on man, you know I haven't seen my daughter in a long time, and I have had this leave scheduled for months. How was I supposed to know we would be working on a jet like this?"

"I know. I am just giving you a hard time. Go have fun man."

"If this jet is still in the hanger when I get back I am going to kill you." I joked.

"If this jet is still in the hanger when you get back I am going to kill myself." He said as we laughed.

Just then one of our flight chiefs, Master Sergeant Cassidy, came out into the hanger.

"Hey Altobelli, can I talk to you in my office for a second?" He said with a nervous look on his face.

"Yes Sir" I replied as I followed him into his office. "What's up?"

"The commander just denied your leave." He said as I stood there in silence. I was looking at him, and he was staring at me seeing the tension and frustration build up inside of me.

"He said your leave balance is short by a day."

"You said I was good. You already approved it and told me to buy my plane tickets. I leave in the morning." I said, feeling my blood begin to boil.

"I know. I am really sorry."

"It's one day, and I am not getting out of the Air Force anytime soon, so you know I will earn it back within the next month. Why can't he just let me go in the hole a day?"

"He doesn't like to do that."

"Sergeant Cassidy. I haven't seen my daughter in 8 months. I am going to be on the plane tomorrow, and I will be back in two weeks. If my leave isn't approved, then you can meet me at the

Airport when I get back with security forces and arrest me for going AWOL. I need to see my daughter. I'm sorry. I am going." I still can't believe I said that. I also was surprised at his reaction.

"Let's take a ride." He said as he grabbed his car keys.

I followed him to his car. We started to drive towards the Squadron commanders building. I knew that he was about to go to bat for me. I had always worked hard for the squadron, and he respected me, and I also respected him, so he showed me that day what he was willing to do for his troops. We walked into the commander's office, and he told me to stay silent.

"Sir, I am here with Airman Altobelli. I had already approved his leave and told him to buy tickets. The oversight of him being short one day was mine, and he should not be punished for it."

My commander just gave him a look and collected his thoughts. It's as if he was lining his insults up in order before he fired them off. I spent the next five minutes listening to my commander destroy Master Sergeant Cassidy, and he just stood there and took it for me. I did not say a word. When he was done yelling at him, he approved my leave, and we went back to his car. We sat there, and I spoke first.

"I'm sorry."

"It's ok. Wasn't the first time I've been chewed out before. It was worth it. You are a really good Airman, and I am not going to lose you over a clerical error."

"I really appreciate that, sir."

My respect for that man doubled that day. I made a promise to myself that I would work extra hard for him and stay late and volunteer for whatever he needed to be done. I now knew that he cared about his troops and was the type of leader that would do anything for them, even if it meant he would get in trouble.

The next day I got on a plane to New York, where I would finally see my daughter. I did not tell anyone I was coming other than my parents and Alyssa, so I did not feel obligated to go and see my massive family while I was home and I could spend time with my daughter. As I sat there on the plane, my demon decided to come out and play. He showed me what it would look like if the plane crashed. The feeling I would get as we plummeted towards the earth to our inevitable doom. The sense of anxiety and uncertainty that awaits us as we wonder what happens next after we close our eyes for the final time. Ever since that day I have a recurring nightmare where my plane banks too hard, and we tumble upside down as the sky now looks like the ground getting larger and larger until finally, I wake up. I never actually crash in these dreams, but I always come close, and they feel so real. This has not stopped me from flying.

I landed in Rochester, New York and the first thing I wanted to do was go see my daughter. My dad picked me up from the AirPort and asked me where I wanted to go. I called Alyssa to ask if I could go get Morgan.

"Hey, I just landed. Can I come to get Morgan?"

"We are busy right now Matt. Maybe tomorrow"

"I haven't seen her in 8 months. I can't come to get her now?"

"No," She said as she hung up on me.

This got me angry, but I decided I should settle in anyways, so I told my dad to take me to my mom's, where I would be staying for the duration of my visit. He dropped me off, and I told my mom what happened. She was upset, but there was nothing I could do at the moment. I went to bed sad that night and had dreams of my daughter. The dream I had would stick in my head for years to come. It was not a bad dream, but one where I could not see my daughters face. It's as if I forgot what she looked like, or maybe she no longer looked the way she once did. Either way, I knew that the last 8 months she did not know who I was, and I was uncertain how she would be with me when I saw her.

The morning came, and I called Alyssa.

"Hey, can I come to pick Morgan up?"

"We are taking her to the beach, so not right now."

"She's my daughter, I only have 2 weeks here. I am coming to get her."

"No, you aren't!" She said, and then hung up on me again.

I broke down. I could not stand the thought of my daughter at the beach with Alyssa and another man playing daddy to her. I began to cry and scream, I was flooded with emotions of hate, and anger, but also sadness and regret. I did not know how to feel and had a hard time processing all of those emotions at the same time. My mom did not like seeing me that way and decided to help me get my daughter. She took me to family court to file for temporary custody under the grounds that Alyssa was an unfit mother. To be honest, she is not an unfit mother. She is not the best mother, but my daughter was always taken care of. I just wanted to see her though, so I did not care.

I got the order from the judge and decided to have my dad serve it to her when I picked up Morgan. She called me later in the day and told me to come to get her from the beach. We drove there, and she met us in a parking lot. Alyssa handed Morgan to me, and my dad gave her the packet of papers telling her that Morgan would be staying with me until our court date a week later. Alyssa became infuriated and reached for Morgan and tried to rip her out of my arms. Morgan started to cry. I held on to her tight and Alyssa began to kick me as her boyfriend, and some of his friends ran down to help her. My dad pulled out his phone and held it up. "I am recording all of you!" He yelled as they backed off. Alyssa then said she was going to call the police. The cops came and talked to both her and me and once they saw the judge's order giving me temporary custody, they let me take her and told her that she needed to let me take her and to handle it in court. This was the beginning of a long and hard road in the court system.

I ended up wishing that I never made the decision to get temporary custody, but I had fought so hard to see my daughter that I wanted to make sure I was going to spend some time with her. This caused Alyssa to go to court herself and file a restraining order against me and began to slander me. Accusing me of being abusive, which in part was right, but not to the full extent of what she was saying. I did end up spending some time with Morgan, but most of my leave was spent in court and fighting with Alyssa, so I could not really enjoy it. In the end, the judge gave Morgan back to Alyssa and granted her residential custody, and final say if we could not agree on something. This is something that she used against me time and time again after that day.

My anger and hate for the American "justice" system grew large that day. Let's look at this from a father's perspective. You father a child, and then go fight a war. Your wife is less than faithful and then when you get back decides to leave you. She takes half your stuff, and you have to pay her for at least the next 18 years when all you really want is to live with your daughter. How is that fair? It's not, but according to the United States, it is Justice. These are the rights I fought for though. What a joke.

Leave was over, and it was time to return to work. I went back to Arizona and reported the next day to the shop. I opened the bay doors and to my surprise saw Aircraft 651 sitting there. I turned to Angley.

"Really?" I said

"Really." He replied

"Well, is it almost done?"

"Maybe."

"Okay, that's reassuring. Let's get back to it then."

I went back into work mode and forgot about the outside world. I was able to shut away from the pain for the 10 to 12 hours I was working on Aircraft or bombs, or weapons. I know now that this was just a way to avoid my problems, which would eventually make them worse, but it was a nice mental escape where nothing on the outside mattered because we had to focus on the mission. Another week passed, and we finally finished 651. It went out for a test and still had the same exact problem it had when we first started working on it. Let me tell you a little bit about Aircraft 651.

Initially, it was firing off its bombs from its triple ejection rack (TER) out of sequence, or intermittently. This apparently was a problem, so they sent our crew to investigate. We ran some tests and decided that we needed to swap out the TER, and it should fix the problem. Sometimes the equipment goes bad, and you need to swap it out and take it to back shop to get repaired. It should have been a 10-minute job. Instead, a car with two civilian contractors came out to take a look. They opened up some panels and decided that the wires were chaffed, and it was causing the unwanted charges that were dropping the bombs. Morris, at this time, was pretty upset and walked back into the flight chief's office. The flight chief on shift I believe was Master Sergeant Bell.

"Why are there contractors out at my aircraft?" Morris asked.

"This jet has been causing us problems for some time, so we thought it would be good to get a second opinion," Bell replied.

"It's the TER"

"Is that what they said?"

"No, they want us to replace hundreds of feet of wiring."

"Then that's what we are going to do."

"It's the TER! Can't we at least try that first?"

"These contractors get paid a lot of money to know what they are doing, let's listen to their advice."

Morris turned and walked out of the office. Although we heard the whole conversation, he turned to us and said, "Okay, we are going to replace the wiring." In such a calm voice that you would never be able to tell he was upset. He was good at that. He never talked negatively about supervision, or orders even if he didn't like them, and he was professional and taught us to get the job done.

After months of rewiring 651, and having it still have the same problem Morris turned to the flight chief and said, "Can we replace the TER?"

"Go replace the TER," Bell replied.

We went out and replaced it, and wouldn't you know it, it fixed it. You would think that this would be the worst part of the story, but it is not. A week later Aircraft 651 was scheduled to leave to get a C mod upgrade. This meant that they would be replacing all the analog systems with digital systems and essentially rewiring the whole jet. The day 651 left we sat out on the flight line. The Aircraft taxied by us, and Angley flipped up his middle finger to salute the Aircraft off. He hated that jet more than any of us. Morris just laughed, and we continued to work.

I continued to work for the Air Force, each day exactly the same, each day missing my daughter more and more. The days grew longer, as our job became increasingly difficult with a squadron merger. We now worked 6 to 7 days a week, 12-hour shifts, for months. It did keep my mind off the fact that I was alone, and my daughter was far away. However, I became burnt out and tired. This was not good for my mind. I felt like I was in an endless loop of doing the exact same thing every day for 6 months. I was going crazy and wanted out. Then a miracle happened. Master Sergeant Bell called me into his office.

"Altobelli, how are you doing?"

"I am ok sir."

"That's good, that's good. So, hey, remember when we talked about you going to work on helicopters?"

"Yes sir, that was a while back, I just assumed it wasn't going to happen. Why?"

"Rescue has an opening. You want it?"

"Are you serious? Yes, I want it!"

"You know they deploy a lot, right?"

"I don't care. I will go."

"Ok, I will give them a call and get you transferred."

"Thank you, sir."

I finally had an out. I would be doing something different, and it felt good. The next day he told me that I would be transferring in two weeks, and I needed to out-process the squadron. I got to work getting all my stuff in order and getting ready for my move to rescue.

Chapter 4

THESE THINGS
WE DO

There were three A-10 Squadrons on base. The Bulldogs, which was the operational squadron, and then two training squadrons, the Lobos and the Dragons. I was in the Lobos. Our Group commander, who was in charge of all three, decided he would try to make his mark on the base before his time as commander was up. He proposed a Super Squadron. Not like anyone could argue with him because it was his call no matter what. What this meant was all three squadrons would become one. This was a bad idea. We spent the next month preparing for the merger. Now you would think that they could just say that we all merged and keep everything physically the same. This was not the case. Each squadron building would belong to a shop now. There was the Crew Chief building, the specialist building, and the weapons building. Everyone had to move, and we had to move all our equipment as well.

This was an enormous task and required a lot of work, so we were all put on 12-hour shifts, and weekend duty until it was complete. Or at least that's what they told us. This also meant that we went from being responsible for 20 jets to 77. We were still split up into maintenance and load crews. I was still on a maintenance crew. I was a Senior Airman at the time, and they decided to give me a crew. I was one of only two Senior Airman to get qualified, and run a crew, the other being Madrid. What happened to Morris and Angley? They PCS'd. Angley got orders to Aviano in Italy, which is where I had tried to get stationed my whole career, and Morris went to Alaska. I was still stuck in Arizona. I had put in for orders and even got to the point where I put worldwide extended long on my dream sheet, which meant I was willing to go anywhere for any amount of time. I was sick of Arizona at this point and wanted to see some new landscape.

They gave me a couple Airman that no one wanted. One of them actually got arrested after I left for stealing motorcycles and running a chop shop. He had recently lost some rank, and they gave him to me. We were in charge of the "7 days" basically I would have to go to all the jets that hadn't been inspected in 7 days and check their gun system, and lubricate the system if needed. I would then have to sign the inspection off in the forms. It was not a very hard job, but it was important. Once I caught a lube line that was disconnected, as the pilot was getting ready to start up the jet. He was scheduled to fire. I pointed it out and fixed it on the spot, so he could still fly. If he had shot, the gun probably would have overheated and possibly exploded, which happened a couple times before. The job itself would typically not take that long back when we only had 20 jets, but now we had 77, so it took an entire 12-hour shift to get through all of them and update all the aircraft forms, and a computer program.

Our 12-hour shifts and weekend duty went on for 6 months. We were getting burned out, so when MSgt Bell, asked me if I wanted to be transferred to CSAR (Combat Search and Rescue) I jumped at the opportunity. I would be working on the minigun and .50 cal on the helicopters (HH-60). It took a while for them to actually get the paperwork done to send me, but finally, the day had come.

On my first day, I walked up to the weapons shop and tried to open the door. It was locked. There was a keypad on the door that you could punch a code in to unlock the door. I did not have a code, so I knocked. The door was opened by an Airman with a 9mm Barretta pistol holstered under his arm.

"Can I help you?" Asked the Airman.

"It's my first day here. I am transferring from A-10s."

"Let him in" I heard a voice say from inside. "Welcome Airman Altobelli. I am MSgt Rose, the flight chief. It's good to have you."

"Thank you, sir," I said.

"Let me introduce you to who we have in the office right now."

There were not that many people in the small weapons room when I got there because most of the squadron was deployed but scheduled to come back in a few weeks. One of the first things I noticed when walking in was the giant vault door that stood in front of me. The procedure to open the vault was intense. You needed to enter a code, call the security forces desk, and they would give you a code word, and you had to reply with the proper countersign, and then you could access the vault. Inside the vault it looked like a man's perfect closet. There were our hand weapons like our 9mm, and M16, and our mounted weapons like the Gau-2 minigun, and Gua-18 .50 Cal.

It was explained to me that the reason we needed to be armed was that all our weapons were man-portable, and if anyone tried to take them, it was our job to get it back. We were the security for the CSAR part of the base. I thought that was pretty cool. It was something different, something new. The shop itself was more laid back than I was used to, and everyone seemed to get along. Almost everyone was on a first name basis which was unheard-of where I came from. It looked like a fun place to work, even though we knew the seriousness of our mission. People's lives depended on us to do our job right. I mean they always had, to some degree, but now more than ever.

The next month I would spend in-processing and getting all my qualifications out of the way. I would go to a two-week course to get spun up on the mechanical and electrical components of the weapons systems I would work. I would go to the range to shoot and qualify on the pistol. Up until now I had only ever fired a rifle, and pistols proved to be a bit harder. I remember the first time I went to chamber a round I rid the slide forward and cut my thumb open. I played it off because I felt stupid that I did that, primarily because I was a weapons specialist and knew better. I still managed to qualify on my first attempt with a pistol, which I was proud of. We had people in our shop who took three chances to qualify on it. Shooting came naturally to me. Not that it is very hard.

Probably my favorite training was going to Scottsville Arizona for advanced training on the .50 cal, and mini-gun. We would learn more in-depth about them and how they function, how to clear jams or do emergency maintenance, and we would fire them off the back of a truck. That was the best, and I knew that CSAR was where I wanted to be. In all my time in the Air Force, this part of my career was my favorite, and I wish I never left. Not only because of the mission, but the people in the rescue community are like no other. We had a very tight bond.

My direct supervisor was SSgt Mendoza. I knew him from A-10s. He was quality assurance for a while and was always really cool with me. He was a fun supervisor to have. Everyone just called him Doza. The way the weapons shop was set up in helicopters was different from any other aircraft. We didn't really have crews, and our job was both flight line and back shop. We would spend our days in the shop taking apart guns, and fixing them if they needed it, and then going to load them up on an HH-60. Once I was 100% task qualified I was moved to mid shift, which was 11:30pm to 7:30am. This was the best shift to be on.

There were only three of us on shift. Sam led the shift with Kevin and myself. We would get into work as the last two Helicopters touched down for the night, and swings would take the guns into the back shop for cleaning. Then we would go back there, take them apart, clean them, and load them back up. We were usually done with all the work we needed to do by 1am, so often Sam would tell Kevin and me to take off and come back before day shift gets in. We would go to Denny's, drink coffee and eat, and just hang out until the sun came up. Our friend Andy was on swings (the shift before ours), so he would stay up and usually join us at Denny's.

The three of us were inseparable. All three of us were from New York, and we all hung out all the time. Most nights on the weekend we would go to our favorite bar, The Red Garter, and play pool all night, or Andy would throw parties with his two homemade beer pong tables, and we would hang out there and play. Kevin and I were partners, and we were outstanding. Not as good as Andy and his partner, who was a crew chief. One time we joined a tournament. It was an official beer pong satellite tournament, and the winner was supposed to be able to go compete in Las Vegas. Since it was Arizona, we were only allowed to use water, and Vegas ended up throwing the tournament out. We still played though. We got to name our teams. Andy named his "two balls, one cup," and ours was "balls deep." Andy and his partner won the tournament, we went undefeated until we played them. Not necessarily something to be proud of but at the time we had a lot of fun.

We had dubbed ourselves the 3 man wolf pack. Andy was dating a civilian girl at the time named Kim, and Kim's friend Allison was always around. The first time I met Allison was at Andy's house. We were playing Call of Duty, and they came over. She introduced herself as Fal, but I thought she said, Val. I called her Val, and she corrected me. She said it's FAL, like Fail at Life. I laughed, but for the life of me can't tell why she ever said that. No one has ever won at life more than that girl. She became important to me. We always joked and said we were "bffs" and then the irony is we became really close friends.

We would go out to eat together, and she would talk to me about guys she liked, or what was going on in her relationships, and I would vent about my situation, and she would offer advice. She was genuinely a really lovely and caring person, and I became protective of her like she was a little sister. Whenever someone would hurt her, my first reaction was to ask her if she wanted me to go "break their legs?" The Italian mafia side of me came out a bit when it came to my friends and people I cared about. It was with her, and my new group of friends, Kevin, and Andy, I learned that I could care about people again, and people could care about me. I would use this opportunity to try to reinvent myself and turn into someone that I wanted to be. This would only be a mask.

First, I needed to decide who I wanted to be. What qualities I wanted to display. I was really enjoying having these new friends and being invited to parties. The group of people I hung out with was like a fraternity, so I guess I turned myself into a frat boy. Every weekend we would go hang out somewhere and drink. We would not just have a couple of drinks, we would drink all night. It usually ended in me throwing up and passing out. Kevin and I had an advantage though. We were on Mid shift, and used to staying up all night, so we could outlast most of the party and drink until the sun came up. (Not necessarily something to be proud of)

Most people drink to forget their problems, and to a degree, it might have been what I was doing. The only problem was that at the end when the room was spinning, and I was on my way to an unconscious state, I would realize that I was alone. No one really loved me, and my past was not going anywhere. I would see images of what I had done before I passed out and re-live that day in my nightmares. Every time I reached that point I wanted to die, and every time I drank too much I thought it could happen, and that would be fine. It would make me angry, and sometimes I would lash out. I tried my hardest to control it, but sometimes it got the best of me.

Time continued forward, and once again I had gone a while without seeing my daughter. She was the person who could keep me grounded and pull me back to reality when times were hard. I missed her, so I decided to call Alyssa.

"Hey," I said as she answered.

"Hi"

"How's Morgan?"

"She is good. She misses you."

"I miss her too. I have been thinking."

"About what?"

"Moving back on base, and maybe having you and Morgan come live with me."

"I don't know Matt. Is that really a good idea?"

"I don't want Morgan to grow up not knowing me. I can be better. Please. Let's just try one more time."

She agreed and a couple weeks later would move back to Arizona with Morgan. We would have a 2-bedroom ranch on base and could try to be a family again. I knew this was insane. We had been in the same pattern before, many, many times. Why would this time be any different? Well, it wouldn't be. The next night I went into work and told Andy and Kevin what had happened.

"Are you crazy?" Kevin said with a puzzled look on his face.

"Yeah man, that doesn't sound like a good idea." Added Andy.

"Look, guys, I miss my daughter and want her back here. Things aren't going to change that much. You will see. I will still be able to hang out."

(Insert eye roll here)

Don't get me wrong, I would still get to see my friends, and we would get a babysitter and go out together, but no one really got along with Alyssa, even though they tried. I think Alyssa didn't try because she knew I had gone out with these people for a long time, while she had to stay home with Morgan and give up her youth. It made her bitter. She was always bitter towards me, and everything was always my fault. I'm not saying she was all wrong, and yes, some things were my fault, but it can't be possible that it is all my fault. I mean, I was trying.

I still worked Mid-shift and would get home around 8 in the morning and go to bed. Alyssa would try to keep Morgan out of my room so I could sleep, but she would manage to sneak in to say hi to me or give me a hug. I couldn't be mad because she was so cute. Sometimes she would just lay in bed with me. I think she missed me. Those were my favorite times. The ones where I could just relax there with my daughter. I knew she was safe, and I was safe, and I wished time would stop and I could feel that way forever. Unfortunately, time won't stop, and I can't keep her safe forever, and that is ok. I have a theory about chaos. It has the potential to make people strong (unless it breaks them).

Have you ever met someone who had a perfect childhood? The people whose parents stayed together made good money never had any problems. They grew up as the "rich kid" so they had nice clothes and people liked them. They were popular in school, maybe played a sport. Always looked happy. Now let's examine their life as an adult when reality sets in. Have you ever seen something happen to them? I'm not talking about something catastrophic. Just a small problem. Maybe something wrong with the car, or house. Maybe a bill went unpaid. What was their reaction? They did not know how to handle it, right? They flipped out and probably didn't know what to do. This small problem has become world ending to them. Now examine someone raised in chaos. They are well versed in the language of misfortune. When something goes wrong, they know exactly how to handle it. They remain calm and know that it is something temporary and it will pass. The thing about chaos is you can only shield someone from it for so long, so protecting your kids from it when they are young, might have an adverse effect on them when they are adults because they don't know how to handle it. Making your kids solve problems young will help them when they are older. I haven't always been able to protect my daughter. I have seen her cry and watched her get hurt, and I believe that she appreciates the good times more because of it. She is polite and appreciative when people do things for her because she knows they don't have to.

Time went on, and my cycle of chaos continued (Some would call this insanity). It was a cool summer night, or maybe it was fall, or perhaps winter. It was hard to tell in Tucson Arizona. I always joked that there were only two seasons there. Summer and Extreme summer. I wanted to go to my friend's house with Kevin for a cookout and to catch up with some people that I hadn't seen in a while. I told Alyssa I wouldn't be gone long. I had a long week, and I just needed to get out. She started to flip out on me.

"No, you aren't going?" She said with Authority.

"What do you mean? You think you can tell me what to do?" I replied

"I have been home with Morgan all day, I don't want you to go, so you're not!"

"Yes, I am!" I shouted as I began to change.

This was when things turned physical. Alyssa grabbed the TV remote and began to swing it at me. I grabbed her wrists and squeezed…hard. She screamed, so I let go. She then threw the remote at my TV. It hit the screen. I screamed again and grabbed her by her shoulders, slamming her into the wall.

"You could have broken the TV!" I shouted.

She was too frightened to respond. She was crying and trying to get out of my grasp. I vastly overpowered her, and she could not move. I knew what I was doing was wrong, but I could not stop myself. I continued to squeeze her arms until I heard her scream in pain. I then threw her across the room and stormed out. I needed to leave.

This was not the first time an incident like this had happened, and it would not be the last. Before my deployment, I would have never laid a finger on her, but now I was always angry and did not know how to handle it. I became violent often. I would never strike her or slap her. I would just hold her down and squeeze hard, so she knew I was in control. She would be scared of me. A couple times I lost it entirely and held a knife up to her throat. In those moments I would picture her dying, bleeding out from a severed carotid artery, and it would bring me joy. Watching her cry, and struggle to escape, completely helpless, snapped me back into reality and I would let her go and then go lock myself in my room until I calmed down. She had to deal with a lot when it came to me, and I am surprised she kept coming back. I was a monster.

Morgan was already asleep, so I don't think she heard us, or if she did, she didn't make any noise because she was scared. As I left, she threatened to call the police. I went to our friend's house, and Kevin was there. He saw I was upset and I told him what happened. Kevin said he would have my back and tell anyone that I had been there all night. He was a good friend and only trying to protect me. He got me a beer, and we started our night. I tried to forget about what happened, and our friend decided to light off some fireworks. Not really legal to do in his neighborhood, but he did it anyway. We stood in his garage drinking as he set off the explosives. I don't even like fireworks, in fact, they would become a pretty big trigger for me, but I was already in a dark place and did not care what we did that night.

Sure enough, about 30 minutes later a cop car pulled up to the house. I started to feel my anxiety rise because in my head I thought they might be there for me. They weren't. It would have been impossible for them to have known where I was anyways. My head wasn't making logical sense at the time though. They asked us if we had heard anything that sounded like gunshots. Our friend was smooth and pointed down the street. He said he thought it was coming from down there and it did have us scared. The cop bought it and turned to his car. Then he did something I will never forget. He said "Hey officer. I hope you catch that rouge shotgun shooter". It took everything in my power not to burst out laughing. The garage went silent. The cop nodded his head and got in his car and drove away. When he was down the street, we all burst out laughing and quoted him all night.

I spent the night and went home in the morning. Alyssa did not say a word to me when I walked in the door. I went right to my room and laid in bed. A few hours later she came to the door.

"Matt, I bought Morgan, and I tickets home. We are leaving."

I laid silent.

"Did you hear me? We are leaving!"

Still, nothing from me.

"Are you going to say anything?"

I wasn't.

Maybe she wanted me to tell her to stay, or say that I cared, but I didn't. I was unable to feel anything. I knew this meant I would go some time without seeing my daughter again, but I could not ask her to stay, and maybe I didn't care. I did not have control over myself when I got mad, and that is the worst feeling of all. I have avoided confrontation for many years now because I did not know what would happen if I got worked up, so instead, I would give in. This is no way to live. People would see it as a weakness that I let others get away with as much as I do, but I do it for their own protection, as well as mine. One day, I might have it under control, but at this point in my life I did not, so I let her go.

At least I thought I was just letting her go. She left on a payday. We had a joint bank account. Here's a lesson for all you kids out there. NEVER have only a joint bank account. She emptied the account and left me with nothing. I found out my account was emptied the hard way. I went to buy some food, and my card was declined. I checked the app on my phone, and my balance was zero. I called her immediately. Her response was, "you will get paid again. You will live." It didn't really help at the moment when I had no food home and had bills to pay. The assistant flight chief offered to give me a $500 loan to hold me over. He knew I was good for it and would pay it back. I turned it down. Instead, I sold my TV and couch to make enough money to get by until my next paycheck. I would be leaving the base soon anyways, so it seemed like the right move. (I got orders)

It wasn't all bad though. I did have moments where I had a lot of fun. As a combat search and rescue unit, it was important for our pilots and gunners to train in all different types of terrain so we would travel to different places for training missions. We packed up all our gear in a truck and began our 6-hour drive to Nellis Air Force Base, in Las Vegas Nevada. The trip was fun. There were about 8 of us in the van I was in, and we spent the ride talking and joking around. When we got there, we checked in to the hotel on base. We slept two to a room. My roommate was a crew chief, and he drove his own car there, so he had transportation for the 10 days we would be there. Not that we really needed it. We had the van, and we all went places together, so other transportation wasn't necessary.

After we were all checked in, we reported to the lobby to go over the plan. We split into shifts. My shift was from 1100 until 1800. It was an easy shift and was perfect because we would get off work, then go down to the strip and stay there until the sun started to come up, go back to our rooms, and get a few hours of sleep before going to work. There were only two nights on that TDY that I didn't go out, and I went to bed early to recover. I'm not sure if you have ever tried carrying around an 80 pound .50 Cal in the desert heat while hung over, but it's not fun. I was young though so I could handle it.

Our group would go out to dinner, and someone would drop their challenge coin, and I always had mine on me, so I would get a lot of drinks for free. If you aren't familiar with Military customs, then the coin may seem strange to you. It is kind of weird, but it has a pretty cool history. According to the most common story, challenge coins originated during World War I. Before the entry of the United States into the war in 1917 American volunteers from all parts of the country filled the newly formed flying squadrons. Some were wealthy scions attending colleges such as Yale and Harvard who quit in mid-term to join the war.

In one squadron, a wealthy lieutenant ordered medallions struck in solid bronze and presented them to his unit. One young pilot placed the medallion in a small leather pouch that he wore about his neck. (I did the same and put my coin in the pouch that held my line badge) Shortly after acquiring the medallion, the pilot's aircraft was severely damaged by ground fire. He was forced to land behind enemy lines and was immediately captured by a German patrol. To discourage his escape, the Germans took all of his personal identification except for the small leather pouch around his neck. In the meantime, he was taken to a small French town near the front. Taking advantage of a bombardment that night, he escaped. However, he was without personal identification. He succeeded in avoiding German patrols by donning civilian attire and reached the front lines. With great difficulty, he crossed no man's land. Eventually, he stumbled onto a French outpost. Saboteurs had plagued the French in the sector. They sometimes masqueraded as civilians and wore civilian clothes. Not recognizing the young pilot's American accent, the French thought him to be a saboteur and made ready to execute him. He had no identification to prove his allegiance, but he did have his leather pouch containing the medallion. He showed the medallion to his would-be executioners, and one of his French captors recognized the squadron insignia on the medallion. They delayed his execution long enough for him to confirm his identity. Instead of shooting him they gave him a bottle of wine.

Back at his squadron, it became a tradition to ensure that all members carried their medallion or coin at all times. This was accomplished through challenge in the following manner: a challenger would ask to see the medallion if the challenged could not produce a medallion, they were required to buy a drink of choice for the member who challenged them. If the challenged member produced a medallion, then the challenging member was required to pay for the drink.

You didn't want to be caught on a TDY without your coin, or you would be spending a lot of money on drinks. We would challenge people by dropping our coin on the bar or table, and everyone had to pull their coin out. If someone didn't have it, they bought the next round for everyone. If everyone had it, then the challenger bought for everyone.

The more we drank, the more shenanigans we got into. Like climbing up on giant horse statues, to then be chased by overweight bike cops. Or finding an entrance to the top of the Miracle Mile Mall, and then peeing on the roof. Dumb stuff. I will spare you the details of most of that trip, because as they say, what happens in Vegas, stays in Vegas. It was a lot of fun though.

Captain Barry was our Officer in Charge in the CSAR unit. He was a very positive influence on me. He was really down to earth and could talk to just about anyone without letting his rank go to his head. I always appreciated those officers the most. The ones who didn't abuse their power and treated us like human beings. He would lead a couple of our PT sessions each week, and they were always the hardest. He liked to keep us moving and keep us in shape. I wanted to make shirts for the squadron that said, "I survived Captain Barry's PT." I think he influenced me to become a physical training leader (PTL). This is where my love for training other people started. It was also where I got into fitness. To be a PTL, you needed to complete a course. The first half was in a classroom learning about nutrition and how the body works, and the second half was in the gym, and they put you through a hard workout to make sure you could keep up and were physically fit enough to tell others how to work out. It wasn't a hard class to pass, and after I graduated, I was then able to design workouts for the squadron. I was working with an Army recruiter at the time to cross into the Army as a Warrant Officer to fly Helicopters. Warrant Officer School would be very physically demanding, so I trained a lot.

At work, I would do what we called 30 every 30. Every 30 minutes on my shift I would drop and do 30 push-ups and 30 sit-ups. I did this all day and got to the point where I was wearing a weighted vest while doing it. This inspired my shop to start doing it too. It was always funny to see because anywhere we were if the half-hour mark hit we would drop and do push-ups. We could be out on the flight line and then suddenly you would see us descend to the ground and start pushing. In the mornings I would run a 5k before work. I would fill my rucksack up with rocks and run the 5k trail mapped out on the base, ending at the gym and then lift some weights.

What sparked my interest in becoming a Warrant officer for the Army? Why would I want to fly helicopters for the Army? I fell in love with Helicopters working with them in CSAR, and I wanted to do more. I knew how to start them up and sitting in the cockpit felt right. I would spend a couple months getting tests done and meeting with boards to get the position. I would have to write an essay about why I wanted to be an Army Aviator. I passed my flight aptitude test with flying colors. No pun intended. I had to go back through MEPS to make sure I was physically qualified. After MEPS, I would meet with the board. I wore my full-service dress blues, with all my awards. I wanted to impress them.

On the board sat three officers. It was a Major and two Captains. I walked in the door and gave my reporting statement.

"Sir, Airman Altobelli reports as ordered," I said as I stood at attention.

"Have a seat Airman Altobelli." Said the Major.

"We have reviewed your packet, and I have a couple questions for you." He continued. "What makes you want to be a warrant officer in the United States Army? It looks like you are doing well in the Air Force."

"I am doing well in the Air Force, sir. Maybe that is why I want to fly. I want to do more. I feel like I am capable of contributing more to the United States Military, and by becoming a pilot, I think I can do that." I responded.

"Well, that's a great answer. I am going to send a recommendation down to Fort Rucker with your package. I believe that airman make the best soldiers. Good luck Airman Altobelli." He said as he dismissed me.

The only thing I had to do now was wait for the Warrant Officer board to accept me. They sent my package to them at Fort Rucker. This board would not get to meet me. They would review my packet and either approve or deny me. They could only allow a certain amount of warrant officers per cycle. When the list came out, I looked for my name. I was the second non-selected. I called the Army recruiter I was working with and asked him why. He checked the notes, and it said that all the people they selected had prior flight experience. I had none. I thought this was stupid, because I passed the aptitude test, and they were going to send me to a school for 9 months to learn how to fly. They said they would give my application a second look in two weeks. I needed to get some flight time.

Captain Barry got word of this and called me into his office. He talked to me about everything and then threw a headset and a flight book at me. He said, "Find a pilot and get up in the sky." He was very supportive of what I wanted to do, and I really appreciate that. I looked up flight classes for what I needed to get done, and the cost was $2,000! I did not have a spare 2 grand lying around that I could blow for a chance to get picked up. I wish I did, but my dream to be a helicopter pilot was dead. Something that should have really upset me, and in a way, it did, but not in the way I thought it would. This was when I noticed that my feelings had become so dulled they were almost numb. I was starting to get used to being disappointed so often it almost had no effect on me.

I had a plan B though. I had recently attended a briefing done on base about becoming an Air Force Recruiter. For some reason, I thought that was a good idea. My First enlistment was coming to an end, and the only skills I had were related to weapons, and there wasn't much of a demand for that in the civilian world, so I knew I needed to change something. I submitted an application to become a recruiter. While I waited for their decision, I got slotted to deploy. I was supposed to leave In July and go to Kandahar. We had been deployed for a little over a year, and we would just cycle our people in and out every 6 months. I was getting deployed with Andy, so I figured it wouldn't be that bad. I liked all these people and actually looked forward to going. Then one day in June I checked my email. I had been accepted and got a class date. The assistant flight chief was standing right next to me when I got the email, and he saw my reaction. He looked at me and asked what it said. I looked at him and said, "I'm sorry, but I can't deploy. I just got orders." He was a little upset, but happy for me at the same time.

To take these orders, I needed to have retainability, which meant I needed to re-enlist. Who better to do my re-enlistment than Captain Barry? I asked him, and he was happy to do it. Alyssa and I had been talking again. I got orders to a place only an hour away from my hometown, so I figured since our biggest problem was she was away from home, and now I fixed that, maybe we would work out. Plus, I really missed my daughter and wanted her to grow up near her family. Alyssa and my daughter were there for my re-enlistment ceremony. My daughter got to see me swear the oath in front of the flag, and a helicopter, and I believe she was proud of me that day.

Earlier that Year I had tested for Staff Sergeant. The results came out before I left, and I made it! I would have to wait to put it on until March 2010, but at least I knew I was getting promoted. Things seemed to be looking up. Andy and Kevin would throw me a going away party. It was huge, and we played Beer Pong one last time. I stayed up all night because I would be leaving for recruiter school the next day. The sun broke over the horizon, and I started my trip back to San Antonio, Texas where my recruiter training would be. Captain Barry ended up getting promoted to Major, and he deserved it. He was always good at taking care of his people. You could tell he actually cared.

My time in Rescue taught me what it meant to have fun and be close to people again. That it was alright to continue living my life despite all the things that had happened to me and what I was going through. I learned what it meant to have real friends and finally felt like I belonged somewhere. I can't remember why I ever wanted to leave there. My persistent mental illness and overly ambitious nature were probably the determining factors in me wanting to get out of there. I was never good staying in one place for too long and always tried to move forward, even if it was a bad idea. To all my rescue people out there...These things we do That others may live.

Chapter 5

BOY, AM I
ENTHUSIASTIC

The drive to San Antonio took me a little over a day. I stopped for one night in a beat up looking motel before finishing the last 7 hours of the drive the next day. I had a friend from my career field going too. He got there before me and called to tell me what to do when I got there. I arrived on base in the late afternoon and went to base lodging to check in. I would be staying in the navy dorms on base. I had my own room with a TV, and a fridge, my own mirror, and sink, but the shower and toilet were shared with the room next to me. The guy living in the room attached to the bathroom was in the Navy, and there for his tech training. I'm assuming his girlfriend or wife didn't take it so well that he was away because I often heard him yelling on the phone, but I would never find out because I never had an actual conversation with the kid.

I had a day to get acclimated to the base before our class started. I had been here before, but only for basic training.

This time I was here for recruiter school and had free-range of the base. I decided to go for a walk. I walked by my old BMT dorm building, and saw many new trainees and started to get flashbacks of when I was in their shoes. A flood of feelings came over me. I felt for them, but also envied them because they all had a clean slate. A fresh start. Their whole career was in front of them, and they had not yet been tainted by any misfortune. The base was so familiar, but also different. It had not changed, but I had changed, and my perspective on what this place was had changed.

I decided to walk back to my room and get my car. I went to the commissary to get some food for the week. I did not have a full kitchen in my room, and we had access to the base dining facilities, but occasionally I wouldn't want to go there, so I bought quick things to make in my room. Microwavable meals, and bread with sandwich meats. If I didn't want to leave my room to eat, then I wouldn't. This came in handy later, because the dining facilities were usually crowded, and we got an hour for lunch during our training, so often I would go to my room, eat quickly and take a power nap.

The first time I went to the dining facility, there was a long line of Navy trainees. I got in line, and it looked like it was going to take 30 minutes to get through it all. One of the trainees looked at me, in my blues with all my ribbons and rank on my sleeve and knew I was not there as a student like them. He knew I outranked all of them, and yelled out, "make a hole!" He looked at me and said, "go ahead, sir." At that moment I felt respected and honored that they would all move so I could eat first, but I was also humbled because I remember what it was like to be them. I looked at him and said, "No thank you. I am not in a rush, and you guys have less time than I do. You go ahead." They closed up the hole, and the trainee looked shocked. He began to ask me questions about what I was doing there, and what I did before and where I have been. I shared a little about my enlistment and gave him the best advice I could. I wanted them to know that we were a team, and in this together. I was no more critical to the mission than they were, and I was not above waiting in line to eat.

The first day of class had arrived, and I headed for the schoolhouse. I felt full of anxiety and stress as I did not know what to expect. Recruiter school had a reputation for being one of the hardest schools in the Air Force, with one of the highest attrition rates. It had to be hard because we would be representing the entire Air Force in a community without an Air Force base. When people looked at us, they would assume our actions reflected all of the Air Force. The process to even get accepted to be a recruiter was tough. We had to submit our performance reports, and a picture of us in uniform, in a particular way, all of our awards, and an essay. Then we would have to interview with a flight chief and answer a bunch of questions. I knew the schoolhouse would be hard.

Most of the class was memorization. On the first day, we got three books and were told we would be memorizing every word in them. We then got a handout called MATTRESS which stood for Money, Advancement, Training, Travel, Recreation, Education, Security, and Satisfaction. Under each category was ways the Air Force offered these. They handed us this and said tomorrow you will be given a blank one and you need to fill it in exactly how you see it here. We had one night to remember that sheet exactly how it was. I almost have a photographic memory. A lot of times I can look at something, then close my eyes and picture it in my head. This really helped out for this task. There are times a photographic memory is a bad thing, like remembering and picturing trauma, but for this, it was helpful. I recreated the worksheet from memory and passed. A lot of recruiter school was pass/fail, as in you didn't get graded, you either passed the task or failed it. If you failed, you had 24 hours to try it again. If you failed a second time, you would get counseled by the head of the schoolhouse. If he let you stay, you had one more attempt, or he would kick you out of the school. We lost a couple people from our class and had one guy cycle into our class from a class further ahead of us.

We were supposed to stay enthusiastic and full of energy at all times to display a positive image of the Air Force. In fact, every day, at least 3 times a day, usually more, we would have to chant and say "Boy, am I enthusiastic!" It almost sounded sarcastic. There were many days that we weren't enthusiastic, because that class was hard. This taught us to fake enthusiasm because no matter how we were feeling that day, in the real world, we would always have to look the part of the happy Air Force recruiter. I was already good at wearing a mask, so this was not hard for me.

We had a "swear and acronym jar" Any time someone said a swear word or a military acronym you would have to put money in the jar because we weren't allowed to say either around civilians. The military is filled with Acronyms that civilians don't understand. I swear I have had a full conversation in acronyms before. This would confuse ordinary people, so we had to break the habit, and that was how. I was the jar keeper. I would try to get people to slip up, so they had to put money in the jar. All the money went towards a big graduation party for us anyway, so it's not like it was a waste.

For example:

"Hey Sergeant Bazile, what was your job before you came here to be a recruiter?" I said knowing exactly what she did before.

"I worked on AWACS." She responded.

"What did you work on?" I asked again.

"AWACS!"

I stared at her and shook the jar.

"Damn it." She said as she handed me $2

You might be thinking this is a "dick move" but it was all in good fun and nobody minded since again the money would be used for our graduation.

Recruiting had one major rule. Don't touch the recruits. It seems weird, but it happens all the time. Young girls see a guy in uniform who has power and authority, and they try to make a move. Female recruits and hopefuls have inappropriately hit on me, and I had to remind them that this was a professional relationship and could not be anything else. I can see where a weaker man might have been tempted. It reminded me of a sign we had on the fridge when I was a weapons troop that read, "If it ain't yours, don't touch it. If it is yours, don't make anyone else touch it." I think it applies to this as much as it does to food.

An Average day in Recruiter school was very long. We woke up at 0500 and reported for morning PT. We would work out as a group and then have 40 minutes to shower, get ready and be in class. This was no problem for me, but the girls did complain about it. It would be different if we just had to throw on our Airman Battle Uniform (ABU) and report in, but we usually had to wear blues and got uniform inspections often. Appearance and presentation were everything in recruiter school. Not just your physical appearance but how you spoke and carried yourself. We would have to give many speeches during the school. I was not a good public speaker when I first arrived. This was the hardest thing for me to overcome. We had to memorize our speech and give it without looking at any notes. This wouldn't be too much of a problem if they didn't know what I was supposed to say, but we had to hand in our written speech to the instructor first before we gave it, and he would follow along to make sure we said every word. There was a lot of pressure, but by the end of the school, I was so much better at public speaking.

In the world of recruiting you could be thrown up in front of a group of people on any given day and be expected to give a speech, so it was important that we developed this skill. Public speaking is all about knowledge in what you are talking about and saying it confidently. The more I gave public speeches, the better I got at it. It is a skill, a talent, like anything else that with time and practice you can improve.

This point in my life provided a good distraction for me. I was feeling good. The constant memory work and assignments kept my mind busy, so I wouldn't focus on my past, or what had happened to me. I was able to keep moving forward. The cognitive load of Recruiter school made it impossible to focus on anything else. Plus, I would get to do a job I wanted, in a place close to home, and be with my family, and not worry about losing my daughter again. I had learned how to interact with people again, and the people in my class at recruiting school became good friends.

Sometimes life is funny. It will give you brief moments of happiness and thoughts about what life could be like. It will provide you with enough to keep on hoping and not give up. It will push you through those hard times when all you really want to do is quit. There were times when I was living because ending my life would destroy my daughter and her feelings are important to me. I have hope. I have her, and I need to do what I can to make sure her life is good. That is why I am still here. That is my purpose, but also my problem. I recognize that I am not living for myself, and when I think about what that means, I come up empty.

Recruiter school lasted almost 2 months. We went through a lot of labs, where we would have to memorize a script, each one getting longer, and complete it with 100% efficiency. They would throw some curve balls our way, like send in a distraction to see how we would handle it or have the applicant bring up an objection to look at how we overcame it. The school was good. I got certified in Professional Selling Skills (PSS) through Achieve Global. I now had a skill I could use when I got out of the Air Force. I was developing my future. That was the point of all this, wasn't it? PSS also gave me another skill set. The power of manipulation. It taught me how to structure information in a way that people would do what I wanted them to and would believe it was their idea. It is a dangerous power for someone like me to possess, and I would eventually be testing it out as I honed this skill for personal gain.

Alyssa flew down for my graduation. We decided that since I would be moving closer to home, we would try it again. (I lost count of how many times this had happened by now) It's funny because she was never there when I needed her during life, but when there was a time for a celebration or a party, she would show up for the glory. I let her. I wish I could say it was nice having her there but honestly it just caused tension. I was worried that if one of the girls from my class said the wrong thing to me, she would blow up on them or on me and cause a scene, so I stayed quiet and didn't get to talk to my friends. They were kind of upset at me for that, but I was doing what I thought was right at the time because I would have to live with Alyssa, and they didn't.

You might be wondering, as I did, how did my goal go from being a helicopter pilot to an Air Force recruiter? I tried to get into my head to figure this out. They are two completely different career fields with nothing in common. My desire to become a helicopter pilot came from my desire to want to do more for the military. To be a contributing part of the war effort again. I thought if I could fly Blackhawks I could go on some search and rescue missions and save American lives. After I was turned down for that, I quickly shifted my focus to becoming a recruiter. At the root of it all, I might have just wanted to leave my duty station and move on with my life. Even though that squadron made me happy and I had good friends, the base itself brought up a lot of bad memories for me, and I was ready to get away from it. Recruiting was an instrument I used to get closer to home so I could be close to my daughter and family. I thought if I were near them it would allow me to heal.

After graduation, we drove back to Arizona to grab what little possessions I had left and out process the base. I stayed in the base hotel, and my brother and his friend drove to Arizona to help me move. I was doing a DITY move, and the Air Force would pay me $5,000 to move everything myself, so I took advantage of that. Back at the base, they were having a promotion party. They handed me sticky blue Staff Sergeant Stripes to put on my sleeve and walk around for the day. It was an honor to make rank, and I was proud of what I had done. I went into my squadron one last time to say bye and thank you to all of them. Most of my shop was deployed. Andy was in Afghanistan but would send me messages online occasionally. Some of them said he wishes I was there, and they could really use me. I can't help but feel like I let my squadron and my shop down by taking orders to be a recruiter instead of deploying again. Who knows what would have happened to me on this deployment though and what I would have become.

My report in date for my new squadron was September 10th, 2009. I would quickly learn how hard being geographically separated from a base would be. I got to Rochester at the end of August and had a few days to find a place to live. I had the cash from my DITY move to furnish a home, so I drove out to Hornell, where my office would be, every day for 3 days until I found a decent townhouse to live in. It was two stories and had 2 bedrooms and 2 bathrooms. It was perfect for my little "family." I went to a furniture store and bought everything we needed for the house and then spent the next couple days putting it all together. My daughter's room was pink and princess themed. She even had a princess bed because she was my little princess and deserved the best. The drive from Rochester to Hornell took about an hour, so it wasn't that bad.

We got settled in our new house and had a couple more days before I had to check in at the squadron. I was eager to get started, so I went and talked to the recruiter I was taking over for. He was the first and only Airman First class to ever become a recruiter. He came from finance. He had some horror stories and tried to scare me away from recruiting.

"You are going to hate it." He said as I sat in my new office.

"Why do you say that? What is so bad about it?"

"Let me show you," He said as he pulled up a list on his computer. "You see all these names in red? These are the people I have to call today."

I looked at the list, and there were about 70 names on it. Which, as a recruiter isn't a lot of calls to make. I would later learn that red meant passed due.

"That's not so bad," I said

"We also have 23 schools we are responsible for in this area. You have to go to a different one every day, on top of doing all these phone calls and holding at least 3 appointments a day with potential recruits. Be prepared for some long days."

Listening to him talk about how terrible it was didn't discourage me. I figured I have been through worse, and at least I'm home. How bad could it be?

The day came that I needed to report to the squadron. The squadron was located in Syracuse, NY. It was close to a 2-hour drive for me. I woke up early and set off to start my new career field. When I arrived, I had to press a button to be let into the building. The Commander's secretary walked out to let me in. She asked if I was the new guy and I told her yes. She handed me a checklist and took me to the first place I had to go. The Air Force loves its checklists, and it looked like we were getting right to business. The secretary was an older civilian woman. There would be a few civilian employees at the squadron. I went over to operations first and got my training all squared away. I would be given another task checklist that I was going to need to complete over the next year to become a certified recruiter. I met with training and marketing, and logistics as well to get my government vehicle and cell phone issued to me. I then met the commander, Col. Roy. He was relatively new to the squadron too and would be there for the next two years. He was an extremely friendly man who cared for all the people under his command.

"Hi Airman Altobelli, I'm Col. Roy."

"Nice to meet you, sir."

"Welcome to the rough riders. I am pretty new here too so the First Sergeant and the fine group of people we have here will be better at answering your questions than me, but if there is ever anything I can do for you don't hesitate to ask."

"Thank you, Sir, I appreciate that.

It was refreshing, and he was probably one of the nicest commanders I had ever worked for. After the day was over, I was officially checked in at the 313th Recruiting squadron. I was a Rough Rider. B Flight. The Bulldogs. (I know. I was a Bulldog again) My Flight Chief was new to the flight as well so we would be learning this together. His name was MSgt Todd Rich. MSgt Rich had an excellent philosophy on recruiting. If you are doing your job and putting people in the Air Force, he would leave you alone. No need to make a certain amount of phone calls a day or do a certain amount of school visits a week, and load a bunch of leads into the system as long as you had recruits in the system and ready to go when the jobs dropped. I really liked this philosophy. It allowed me some freedom at first.

There were a couple recruiters in the flight that had an impact on me. One was MSgt Clark. MSgt Clark was security forces by trade. He had a hard exterior and came off a little scary to those that didn't know him. He was probably the person in the flight I related to the most. We are both Republicans and believe in hard work and agree on what we think is the main problems of society these days. We would have long conversations about work, and the dumb things that high school kids are doing now. He was into fitness, and so was I. He was also probably the most educated person I met in the Air Force. He had 5 degrees, and could have been an officer three times over but decided to stay enlisted. He wasn't afraid of work and loved what he did. Security forces that is...Everyone had the same feelings about recruiting.

SSgt Tharp was probably one of the more entertaining recruiters. It took him a while to get the hang of recruiting, but he always had a positive attitude and would make jokes. I trained him for the most part, and he would call me for help or advice whenever he needed it. I was always happy to give it because he usually had a funny story to tell me as to why he was asking the questions. Whenever there was a road trip to the flight office, or we had to go somewhere we would drive together and have a good time. It was people like him that made the job bearable.

So, what was so bad about recruiting? Individually the tasks were not that difficult. We would have priority 1, 2, and 3 schools we had to visit. Every day was a different school. We had telephone prospecting we had to do which is basically calling up a parent and saying "Hi, this is Sergeant Altobelli, can I please have your child?" Most of the time you would get nowhere with them, but occasionally you would get the parent of a disabled child who decided to tell you exactly what they thought of you. We would have to hold "center of influence" events, and volunteer in the community. We would have to do all the paperwork to enlist someone and make sure it was perfect, so MEPS didn't kick it back. We then had to brief our recruit on how to get through MEPS and drive them up there and bring them home the next day when they were done (which was a 2-hour drive one way). Everything we did needed to be documented in our planning guide, in its specific binder, and in a computer program called AFRISS. I would have to write down something I did three times. It took longer to document an event than it did to actually do the event itself. All of this would have to be done pretty much at the exact same time. I am only one person. It made it impossible to do everything by the book and still finish every task they asked of me. Trust me. I tried. When I was new I did everything by the book, and one night I was in my office until 1am, and then I had to be back at 6am.

I was never home. I might as well have been deployed for 4 years. 4 years of doing this day in and day out. For every one Air Force recruiter, there are two to three Navy recruiters, four Marine recruiters, and eight to ten Army recruiters. I had to do the job of multiple people, against multiple people, all by myself. I was good at it. I had a good head start though. I was left with 97 overdue follow-ups. Between that and the 120 leads, I got from my first career fair I had a lot of people to talk to, so I began to set up appointments. I remember my first one on one interview with someone interested in the Air Force. I tried to remember recruiter school and the script and PSS, and pretty much followed that. The thing is, ordinary people don't follow a script, so when the kid brought up some drawbacks or had good points that I could not overcome, I froze. I actually said, "I'm stuck." It was recommended that I record my appointments and listen to them after, so I can analyze what I did wrong and what I did right. When you listen to yourself talk and realize you sound stupid, you will do whatever it takes to not sound stupid again. I set up more interviews and held more appointments, made more phone calls, and I got good at "selling" the Air Force. I had a sizeable delayed enlistment program filled with people waiting for jobs. I got to the point where I had 10 to 15 people on my qualified and waiting list, which meant I could take it easy for a while.

I became the squadrons go-to guy for recruiters. I had people willing to do battlefield jobs, and hard to fills. Any time a job came up that no one could take they would look to me to talk someone into it, and I usually did. I made silver badge my first year and was in the running for a gold badge. Why did I do so well? My personal life sucked. Pretty much the whole time I was in the Air Force my personal life suffered, so I threw myself into my work. I was very competitive and liked to be the best at whatever I was doing. Believe it or not, Alyssa and I did not stay together very long after I became a recruiter. I started recruiting in September 2009, and we broke up at the beginning of February 2010. This time for good. That would be it for us. I would never take her back again, even though she tried to come back. I didn't need her anymore. I lived close to my daughter and could see her whenever I wanted. I told her when she was about to leave for her dads that if she left this time, I would not take her back.

Maybe she thought I was bluffing, but I stayed true to my word. Why did we break up this time?

As you know, I had made rank and was about to put Staff Sergeant on the first of March, but first I had to make it through Airman Leadership School (ALS). Since I was globally separated from a base, they would need to send me to Hanscom Air Force Base, in Boston. It was an 8-hour drive from where I lived. I would need to spend a month there, and my class started in January and ended in February. At ALS, we would learn how to be a direct supervisor and be given situations we would have to solve. We would learn about the code of conduct and have to give speeches. I figured I would be good at this because I was a recruiter and had a lot of practice with speeches. We would also be tested on marching a flight. Compared to recruiter school, ALS was a breeze.

I made some new friends in ALS, both a mix of guys and girls. Some of them would text me about assignments or tell me the class was canceled due to snow the next day. Alyssa decided to look up who I was talking too while I was away, and then started to text the numbers that were calling and texting me to see who they were. This caused a lot of trouble for me in class, and everyone was telling me that my wife was calling them and flipping out on them. Naturally, this caused me to get angry and I called her to say what she was doing was very unprofessional. She then threatened to call my commander and tell him I was cheating on her. I wasn't, but she liked to accuse me of it. She actually did e-mail my commander's wife, and when I got back, I had to go meet with my commander. It wasn't only because of that. She had told my commander that I was having an affair with the Olean recruiter, SSgt Delacruz. I wasn't. We were friends, and occasionally I would use her ASVAB testing site and do work in her office while I waited for my recruits to get done testing. Word spread around the squadron, and then there were rumors that we were together. When she became pregnant, everyone assumed it was mine. It wasn't.

A combination of Alyssa accusing me of cheating and trying to get me kicked out of the Air Force, again, led to me finally thinking straight and not wanting to ever take her back. She moved in with her dad, who had room for her and Morgan. I would drive to Rochester on the weekends to see my daughter. I did a lot of driving as a recruiter, so I did not mind the hour drive to Rochester each weekend. It was relaxing and gave me time to think and clear my head. Then when I got there I would get to see my little girl, so everything was great.

The day came for me to put on Staff Sergeant. I went to the local dry cleaner who was in the military when he was younger, and he put my new stripes on my uniform. So, as a Staff Sergeant, what changed? Nothing. In the operational Air Force, my job would have changed, and I would have been a direct supervisor, but recruiting was different. In Recruiting Rank did not matter like it did in the rest of the Air Force. Experience mattered. You would have Tech Sergeant flight chiefs telling Master Sergeant recruiters what to do. If you were an experienced recruiter, you held power. I would be sent to train Master Sergeants as a Staff Sergeant. It was a weird concept to get used to, but it is kind of how the civilian world operates. There is no rank in the civilian world, and experience is how you tell who you listen to. The nice thing about the real Air Force is your advancement follows you. A Staff Sergeant on one base is the same as a Staff Sergeant on all bases, so you never have to worry about being the low man on the totem pole again once you make rank. This did not apply anymore.

I was good at recruiting, so I was not at the bottom for long. I won Non-Commissioned Officer of the quarter, and flight MVP for the year. It felt nice to be on top. My confidence and ego would eventually get the best of me. Once the recruiter left Rochester, I tried to take the office. It was a hard argument to win, but they gave it to me. I wanted it so I could be closer to Morgan. I told them that I was from Rochester and have a lot of contacts and could do really well in that office. The past recruiters had failed at making goal in that office. I did use my contacts and set up events. I set up a lot of appointments and had a lot of interested people wanting to join the Air Force. The problem I ran into was the same problem as the previous recruiters. These people didn't qualify. Between the education gap and law violations, it was hard to get anyone in the Air Force without a waiver. Right here I should have started to notice my pattern of failure. I would get perfect at something, become overly ambitious, overreach, and fail. This won't be the last time (not even close) that I display this pattern.

At this point, I still lived in Hornell. I was still the recruiter there, and I had rented the old Navy recruiters house. It was a large house with three bedrooms and two bathrooms, a porch and a backyard. It was nice but ultimately too big for me. I turned two of the rooms into guest rooms and would often have my friends from Rochester come over, and they had a place to stay. We would go to my favorite bar in Hornell. They had pool tables, and I knew everyone there. The Navy recruiter Mike would always go with us. Mike was a good time. He was hilarious and often tried to be my wingman. I accused him of being the world's worst wingman because he would always try to set me up with crazy girls, or ugly ones, but Mike was gay, so maybe he just didn't know any better. I know what you are thinking. A gay guy in the Navy. Pretty Cliché, right? I never let him forget it. He was a very good friend of mine though, and we would help each other out at work. I sent him a lot of recruits who didn't qualify for the Airforce, and occasionally if one of his did, he would walk them over to me to look at all their options. He was a good guy and cared about his job.

Being alone, in a big party house, right down the street from my favorite bar was not healthy for me. I would get into my head a lot. When I was alone, I felt paranoid and feared the worse. Every bump in the night or creek of the old house was someone breaking in to kill me. One small thought would grow in my head until I could clearly hear voices coming from the downstairs. That is why I spent many of my nights at the bar and would usually end up bringing company back to the house. Sometimes it was one person, or sometimes I would just invite most of the bar back to keep the party going. Anything to avoid being alone with my thoughts. I was like the poor man's Great Gatsby. The company of strangers felt lonely to me as well. It no longer helped the situation, and instead, I became paranoid about those people. What would they do to me while I slept? I would stay up and often scare my house guests. I felt the need to make a real human connection, and not just drunk ones.

After about a year of recruiting, I took a couple weeks of leave. Most people when they take leave they go home, and away from a base. I was already home and missed life on a base, so I took leave and decided to visit my friends in Arizona. I flew out there and was picked up by Fal. There were not too many people left in the area when I came back. Kevin lived in Phoenix, but he drove down to Tucson to see me. Most of the time I was there I hung out with Fal, Sam, and Bobby. I even saw Kim once while I was there. Kim and Fal now had a strange relationship. They were really close until Kim and Andy broke up.

I am not exactly sure what happened, and I didn't feel like taking sides. Kim never did anything wrong to me, and I still saw Fal as one of my best friends, so I would stay out of it, and Fal did not get me involved in it which I respected. She and Andy were not yet together at this point, so it wasn't over that. However, I did find it Ironic that she ended up Marrying Andy, who was Kim's ex-boyfriend. It could have been a soap on daytime TV. There wasn't really a lot of drama about it or anything else for that matter. We all just liked to have fun.

When I was in Arizona, I began to talk to a girl who lived in New York and sent me a message on Facebook. We started to talk, and I ended up asking her out to dinner when I came home. It's so funny how something as small and innocent as a Facebook message from a stranger could turn out to be something that largely impacted your life. At the time she messaged me because her sister went to school with my cousin. I talked to Fal about her, and Fal told me not to trust her. She was protective of me like I was with her. I didn't listen to Fal, but I probably should have. I should have seen the warning signs by the shallow compliments she was giving me. She would say things like "I like big biceps" and complement my physical features but not much else. I chalked it up to her not knowing me yet though, so how could she compliment anything else?

The day I got back to Rochester was the night of our first date. I got ready and went to pick her up. I am the type of guy who walks up to the door and rings the doorbell when I pick someone up. Call me old-fashioned, but it is the right thing to do. I parked my car and got out, but she must have been watching for me because she came out of the side door of her house. I took her out to a nice Italian dinner. We did the standard first date and talked about what we did. I told her I was in the Air Force and a recruiter, and she talked about school, and what she wanted to do with her life. She had a one-year-old daughter and spoke highly about her, and her family.

Why I brought this up is because she would usually drive down to Hornell to see me. She was my first serious girlfriend after Alyssa. She would work around my schedule so we could spend time together. I eventually met her daughter, and she met mine. I was funny about that. I didn't want anyone to meet Morgan unless I knew they were going to be in my life. The first time she met Morgan was at the beach. We met each other there with our kids, and they played on the playground. We wanted to make sure they would get along. They did. I believe Morgan could get along with anyone though. Her daughter was incredibly cute too, so it helped. She was a hilarious little girl. At such a young age, she had such an old personality. I ended up loving that little girl like she was my own.

When I moved to Rochester, I got a townhouse with my new girlfriend. It had two rooms, so one of them we turned into the girl's room. We put two beds in there and then turned the basement into their playroom. The whole house ended up being their playroom, but it was a nice thought to try to isolate all the chaos into one room. I thought that this might be it for me. My family for the rest of my life and Morgan would grow up with a sister and be really close. That was my plan anyway, but it didn't work out like that.

My girlfriend's car died. It would not start anymore, and she could not get it fixed. It was an old beat up car anyways, so what did I do? Here, you can have my car. Yes, I gave her my car and went and bought a new one. I should have got a practical car, but that would have been smart, and I made some insane decisions. I don't think I was capable of making rational choices at the time. The sensible part of my brain was damaged by the demon who lived inside of me. I bought a RED 2011 Dodge Charge RT, with a Hemi. It was $36,000. I could afford it. I made good money as a Staff Sergeant recruiter in the Air Force. The purpose of giving her my old car was so she had transportation to and from school. She ended up dropping out of school when we moved in together. She didn't know what she wanted to do and made me promise her one thing. She asked me to promise her to not let her do nothing with her life. I agreed.

PART 2
CONSEQUENCE

Chapter 6

FREEING A CAGED DOG

In the beginning, things were ok. I would go to work, and my girlfriend would stay home with her daughter. She was no longer in school and was between jobs, so she made her priority raising her daughter. I helped her with her daughter from the time she was only 1 year old. I was there for her whenever she needed me. I made enough money to cover all our bills, so I didn't mind her staying home. After about 8 months of living together, depression set in. She wasn't in school and didn't have a job. She stayed home all day and complained that she was gaining weight, so I got her a membership at planet fitness. I even offered to go with her to the gym and train with her. I did a couple times, but she became disinterested in that too. She was stuck in a rut. Something I had been in time and time again. I reminded her of the promise I made her when we first moved in together. She started looking for a job, and I thought everything was going to be ok. She ended up getting a job as a waitress at a bowling alley, working nights, and would often not get home until after Midnight. I would watch her daughter at night and put her to bed. I didn't mind it, and she was good for me. It gave us time to bond, and I enjoyed spending time with her. Then when she was asleep, I would get some time to myself to play video games or watch a movie.

My girlfriend made some new friends at the bowling alley. Some nights after work she would go with them to a bar for a couple drinks. I never got invited to go out with her, and many times she wouldn't even tell me she was going. I remember one night I rented some movies for us to watch and made food for her, and she did not come home when she said she was. I tried to call her, but her phone was off. She got back a couple hours later and said she went out for drinks and left her phone in the car. We began to grow apart and fight a lot. She always put herself down, and I would try to tell her she was wrong and had a lot going for her. She would tell me to shut up and didn't believe me. She told me I had to say that because I was her boyfriend, and began to look for compliments from other people. Other guys. I had a bad feeling in my stomach like something was wrong.

One day I came home from work to a much emptier townhouse and a letter on the table. The message was really nice, honestly, but I did not care. It said how she feels she wasn't good enough for me and wanted to go back to school and do things on her own before she could be with anyone. She said that maybe one day we would be together again. I called her immediately, but she did not answer. It took me a long time to get a hold of her. I called her mom and sisters and tried to figure out where she was. Finally, she called me back and ended up hanging up on me. I could not believe she did this to me. This was the event that started a spiraling effect downwards to a familiar place labeled Rock Bottom. The hardest part about this was losing her daughter too. I looked in her room, now basically empty, and it reminded me of when I lost Morgan for those 8 months. My brain went back to those dark times, and I began to slip. I started having panic attacks again and blacking out. I became unreachable. I became a tornado again and wanted to destroy lives. So, I did.

My now ex-girlfriend's friend spent some time with me and tried to get me out of the house. She offered me some interesting information.

"Matt, you are too good of a guy to keep this from." She said

"Keep what from?"

"When we would go out after her shift she got drunk and asked me to drop her off at this guy's house. She spent the night there."

I fell silent. I did not know how to react. This did not help me come back from my insanity and instead drove me deeper and deeper into darkness. I started to wonder why I wasn't good enough. Of course, I am not good enough. I don't deserve happiness. Everything I love ends up leaving. I went mad.

I confronted her about it, but she swears nothing happened. I don't believe her, but it doesn't matter anyway. The relationship was apparently over. Deeper and deeper I dove into madness. I started to do crazier things. I put a mask on and grabbed a gun and went to where she worked now. I waited in the dark for her shift to end. I was not sure what I was going to do when I saw her. Why did I even bring the gun? If something happened to her, they would know it was me. What saved me from making the biggest mistake of my life that night was a picture I kept on my dash in the car. It was a picture of Morgan when she was a baby. If she ever found out that her father was a killer, she would never forgive me, and I would never be able to see her again. I put the gun in my glove box but did not leave. I watched as she walked to her car. She got in, and I walked up to the window.

"Matt, what are you doing here?" She asked

"I don't know. I wanted to see you."

"Just go home."

I went home and started to think about how crazy I was. I remember the night she came back to get her stuff and how that conversation went. I tried to convince her to stay and became hysterical with rage. On an impulse, I reached for my gun, with the intent of blowing my head off. As I grabbed it aggressively, it slipped out of my hands and flew across the room landing under my desk. She did not see what it was I threw. I frantically looked for it but was unable to find it. I planned to kill myself in front of her and ruin her life. Obviously, that was a bad plan, because I would only be ending my life, but I had no impulse control. I was lucky that I lost the gun that night and didn't find it until after I had calmed down and moved my desk.

The thing about suicide is that in order to commit it, you need to believe your life is worse than death. The phrase "every day is a blessing" gets thrown around a lot by the privileged American people who have all their needs and wants satisfied. This is not how the majority of the world lives, and they do not see every day as a blessing. They see it as a curse. Take the radical terrorist. To commit the crimes they do, they have to not only be willing to die but to incorporate it into their plan. Take an objective look at their life though. They come into the world knowing struggle. Poor living conditions, in hot temperatures with stringent religious views. To them, the promise of a Utopian afterlife outweighs the fear of death. They don't have anything to preserve here on Earth, so giving their lives for their God in hopes of reward is an easy choice. Americans have a life worth preserving and will fight to live in most cases. I think the reason

22 veterans commit suicide a day is that they have seen what it is like to give up everything for their country and be rewarded with nothing but mental issues, loss of limbs, and chronic pain. We need to do better.

Weeks have passed, and the people that cared about me tried to get a hold of me but could not. I was not myself. I did not answer any phone calls. I was too busy destroying all my stuff and making a mess in my townhouse. Finally, my father had come over to check on me. The scenario now reversed from when I was a child and went to check on him when we didn't hear from him. I had become my father, only worse. I was in the townhouse when he opened the door. I don't remember unlocking the door, but I must have because he walked in, and I was passed out on the couch. He looked around.

"Matt, what happened in here?" He asked

I stayed silent.

"People have been trying to get a hold of you. Why aren't you answering your phone?"

"I was sleeping."

My dad now sat next to me on the couch.

"Tell me what is going on."

"I can't," I replied

"Yes, you can. You can tell me anything. You know I have been where you have been before, and I know how it feels. I just want to help you."

"It is not the same thing."

Eventually, I broke down. I told him what had happened in Afghanistan and what was going on in my life. He began to cry, as he felt bad for me and the pain I was going through. He started to blame himself for the way I was, but it was not his fault. I was sick. I had a sickness, and it needed to be dealt with. I was ready to get help.

At this point in my life, I was not only dealing with a mental illness but a physical one as well. Years of exposure and all the things I put my body through had finally caught up to me. I also thought it could be a physical manifestation of the stress I was going through. My issues were on my skin and in my lungs. Any small cold, or sickness, or any bacteria exposed to an open wound would render me incapacitated and hospitalized. I would get massive legions on my face, and skin, and feel physically ill. The worst one was a growth on the side of my face that grew so large, the pressure was almost unbearable. The proximity to my head and brain gave me intense headaches, which would cause me to vomit and lose consciousness. The pain already felt like a bullet was lodged in my head, so I toyed with the idea of actually putting one there.

I ended up in the hospital, and the nurse was supposed to administer morphine. The pain did not dull. The Doctor thought I was lying. The Doctor himself ended up delivering stronger pain medication. Weeks later I would be approached by a detective who told me the nurse was stealing narcotics and selling them, so what he actually pushed through my IV was saline and not morphine. Such was my luck.

Events like this would happen once or twice a year after I got home. It became normal, and I grew better at seeing the signs and catching it early enough to avoid any widespread pain or discomfort. The pain medication was always something I looked forward to when I was hospitalized. It would numb me, both physically and mentally. For the hours that I was under the influence, I would not have to deal with my mental demons or the physical world. I could escape. I could see how people could get addicted to these. Lucky for me I don't have an addictive personality when it comes to substances. I would take all the pills prescribed to me, even if I didn't need them, but once they were gone, I did not try to get more. I did not feel an excessive need to keep taking them. Besides, I was sure that I would be hospitalized again in a few months anyway, and at that time they would prescribe me more.

The physical illnesses I endured were almost like a break to me. It gave me a chance to slow down and get some much-needed rest. As messed up as it sounds, I almost enjoyed it. I got to catch up on sleep and have a somewhat regular schedule. I would not need to worry about work for a few days or a week, depending on how long the Doctor recommended I stayed out of work. The physical illness could also be dealt with, and then it was gone. It was so much easier to get rid of than the mental illness. I would eventually get to find this out in the hardest way.

My talk with my father was around the beginning of December. After that, I went to my primary care physician. I told her what was going on, and she told me that we were going to try a series of medications until we found one that worked. I would need to be taken out of work until we found one that works because the side effects of the medication could make it dangerous for me to drive, or even be out of the house. The Air Force reluctantly placed me back on quarters, and my flight was given strict instruction not to bother me with work questions until I was better.

At first, I was given 3 medications. One for anxiety, one for depression, and Xanax for panic attacks. The Xanax never lasted long. That night I took all three. I realized that life was going to get a lot harder before it got any better. I became disconnected from myself. I began to have terrible dreams and hear things in my townhouse that were not really there. I began to torture myself again and became paranoid that someone was going to come and kill me. This was also the first time I was able to process the death of my grandfather. It was something that should have shaken my world at the time that it happened, but it didn't. I couldn't even cry. Now all those emotions came flooding through as I called out for him. I wanted to see him and talk to him again. He would have the answers for me. Part of me thought I was going to die and see him again soon, and that gave me a temporary comfort until I remembered that I didn't really believe that. I fell asleep. I stayed asleep.

This lasted for about 3 days. I did not get out of bed. I heard a knock on the door. It was increasing in volume and rhythm. A persistent knock, as if whoever it was had been knocking for a long time. I walked down the stairs slowly, in a fog, and opened the door to see my gym friend standing there. We would typically meet at the gym every morning to workout. I had been absent. He came to check on me.

"Hey, Matt. Haven't heard from you. I tried calling, but you didn't answer. Are you ok?"

"Yeah, I will be ok. I have just been sleeping a lot. This new medication has me pretty down."

"Ok. You up to go to the gym?"

"Not today. I can't drive right now either until I find a medication that works."

"That's ok, I will pick you up."

"Ok. Let's shoot for tomorrow then."

"Sounds good. Get some rest man. I will see you in the morning."

I shut the door and crawled back up the stairs to my room. Slow and dizzy. I thought to myself how difficult it would be to lift anything right now. I took my pills and went back to sleep.

I ended up going to the gym the next morning in an attempt to get back into a routine. I thought it would help me get my sanity back. I went back to the Doctor and told her that these pills weren't working, and she prescribed me another one. I took it right away. I had multiple medications running through my veins and counteracting with each other. The results were terrifying to me. My demon played games with me. He would show me death, and send more noises, and voices. People yelling, weird sounds, paranoia. It was hell on earth, but I battled through it and tried to appear as healthy as I possibly could. My demon would also show me images of my ex with other men, and toy with my emotions. It would force me to vomit, sometimes throwing up the medication I had just taken. My stomach began to hurt bad, and I was taken to the hospital early one morning. The same image kept going through my head of my ex and another man. I could not shake it.

December seemed to last an eternity. It felt like one very long day. I can't remember most of it, but I know it was slow. I don't even remember what I did for Christmas, or if I got my daughter anything. I don't remember seeing her, and I kind of hope I didn't, because I did not want her to see me that way. New Years was quickly approaching, and I was invited to a party. That night would prove to be one of my worst. I got there and was handed a drink. Alcohol does not mix well with all the medication I was on. I knew that, but at the time I did not care. I drank a lot that night. We went out into the garage, and we fired up the grill to cook some sausages. My buddy had gotten a couple Cuban cigars, so we lit them up and continued to grill. Fireworks were going off, and this gave me a "great idea." (Hold my beer) I had my pistol in my car, so I went and grabbed it and walked back towards the garage.

"What are you doing?" asked my friend

"With the fireworks going off no one will notice if we fire this off into the air. Want to shoot it?"

"Hell Yeah!" He said as I chambered a round and handed it to him.

He pointed the 9mm pistol to the sky, and fired off one shot, threw the gun at me, and ran inside. I was still calm, and no one was outside, so I walked out to the yard, pointed it in the sky and fired off a few more rounds. It felt good, but also reminded me of why I was on all this medication, to begin with. I walked back to my car and put the pistol back in my glove box.

I was drunk, grilling sausages with a Cuban hanging out of my mouth and firing my 9mm into the air. This was probably the most gangster I was or will ever be. It gets worse. As the night continued I drank more and was having a good time. I then get a text message from a girl who I worked with at a program for the boy scouts of America. I ran a program for them where we would take kids interested in different career paths and teach them about the Air Force. She also worked with me on the STEM initiative to increase interest in Rochester's Youth.

She asked me what I was up to. Before that night we had always been professional, and if I were sober, I probably would have remained that way. She told me she was at a party and didn't have a ride home. She was obviously intoxicated too and said I should come and get her. I told her I was at a party too, but I could drive. I was in no condition to drive. I should have just gone to bed. I decided to go to the party she was at, and entered the address in my GPS and headed out. It was downtown Rochester NY, on a night where there were more cops out, and checkpoints than any other night. I must have passed a dozen cops, but I did not get pulled over. I made it to the party and went inside. She greeted me at the door with a drink. She introduced me to all her friends, which I don't remember a single one of them. In fact, right after this point, I can't recall much of anything.

What I do remember is waking up at 0500 at her place. I was in a panic because I don't know how I got there, or where I was or what was happening. She was a little freaked out and asked if I was ok. I said no and told her I had to leave. I walked outside and got in my car, drove home and went to sleep. I felt terrible. That night was probably the most reckless night of my life. I could have gone to jail, or hurt someone, or killed myself, or killed someone else. All the possibilities ran through my head, and I decided that I was better off staying in my townhouse alone, and not associating with people. I wasn't even supposed to be driving. What was I thinking? That I didn't care what happened to me anymore because I did not want to live. I did not want to kill myself either, but if it happened, I wasn't going to be too upset. It was a selfish thing to do. I have a daughter who loves me more than anything, and it would have broken her heart if I died. It also would have made her hate me if she found out how. Maybe that's what I wanted. If she hated me, it would be easier to lose me. I am not sure. This period in my life was messed up, and it gets worse.

Over the next couple of months, I would be switched to 6 different medications. Not giving one time to exit my body before starting the next one, sometimes being on two or three of them at the same time. It made me sleep. A lot. I would sometimes sleep for an entire day. I continued to hear and see things that weren't really there. One night I woke up because I thought I heard a voice. I looked over to my door and saw what I could only describe as the grim reaper. I could just see half of him, the other half behind my door. It was as if he was peeking into my room to check on me. To see if I was still alive or if it was time to take me. This sent my mind wild. I continued to stare at my door, hoping my eyes would focus and it would be a jacket or a hoody hanging up. My eyes did not focus past him. In my mind, he was really there. I felt my blood pressure rise as I began to sweat. I knew a panic attack was coming on and I reached over to the nightstand for my pills. I grabbed the Xanax and took one. When I looked back at the door, he was gone. I would still hear voices, and noises all night, and did not get back to sleep for a while.

People began to worry. My gym partner would come to check up on me from time to time, to make sure I was ok. He was a good friend. One I would eventually lose because I am a tornado. For now, though, he was a good friend, and we had plans to start a business together. We obviously put them on hold while I was going through all this. We had invented something that could change the way people workout. It was kind of like the Fitbit for lifters. We called it the trainer tracker. It still has not been made, and I'm not sure if it ever will be, but for the sake of confidentiality, I will say no more about it. It was our baby, and if I don't finish it with him, then it doesn't get finished.

You can only be alone with yourself for so long until you eventually go crazy and want to talk to someone other than the voices in your head. I got on my computer and went to a website called chat roulette. Basically, it would connect you with other strangers at random from all over the world. You could hit next to talk to someone else. I would spend hours looking for someone to talk to. I met people who spoke different languages, and we would try to understand each other. I was not on there to look for someone to make me feel better. I was on there to talk to anyone. Anyone who would not click next and want to listen or have me listen to them. There were conspiracy theorists on there who would tell me about their theories. There were people on there who just wanted to make fun of you to see if they could get you pissed off. People were looking for someone to love or lust after.

I liked it because I could be anyone. Not one of these people knew me, and after I clicked next, they would never see me again. I could tell them my deepest and darkest secrets, and they could not tell anyone. They would never find me, so it didn't matter. It was my own form of therapy. Eventually that all changed. I met someone on there who lived in Florida, and she was getting too close. She actually wanted to be friends. She eventually wanted to be more than friends. Let's call her X since she told me that her parents didn't name her right away and that is what was printed on her first Birth certificate. Every night I would log on and talk to her. We now had each other's personal information.

"Hi, Matt. I missed you" X said

"Hey, how was your day."

"It was good. I can't wait for this semester to be over. What about you?"

"More of the same."

"Cheer up. So, hey, I have been thinking. Spring break is coming up, and I wanted to know if you wanted to come to visit me? Or I could come to visit you. How does that sound?"

"That sounds good. Just give me the dates, and I will get a plane ticket."

I had no real intention of going to see her or having her come to see me, but I could not tell her that. I don't know why. This thing that was supposed to give me relief had now given me someone that actually cared about me, and I hated it. I had no real feelings for her. To me, she was a picture on a screen. I was not capable of emotions. I played along, but in my head, knew that I wanted nothing to do with her, and would eventually hurt her. It wasn't until a week before her break that I told her I wasn't going to see her over break, and then I abruptly stopped talking to her altogether. People were expendable to me. I wanted nothing from them, but I could not go without interacting with them. They were a playground for my demon to feed. I let him run wild.

The next connection I made on Chat Roulette was a girl who was in a bad situation. She lived with an abusive ex-boyfriend and was trapped. In one day I got her to quit her job, uproot her whole life, and move to NY, only to send her right back two weeks later. I really was a monster. I had no intention of hurting people, but my demon was smart. He would give me just enough emotion to think I could be normal and have a connection with someone, and then I would wake up one day and feel nothing. I would be frustrated that I felt nothing. I only knew that I wanted to be alone until I was, then I didn't.

My squadron and flight chief would call me to check up on me and see how I was doing, and when I would be coming back to work. SSgt Tharp took over my responsibilities while I was away. I'm sure he hated that. He would still call me to ask questions, even though they told him not to, and I would help him out because it was the least I could do for him. MSgt Clark would also call me and talk to me about his situation and try to offer advice to make me feel better. It was nice to know I had people that cared about me and my well-being.

During my "down time" I had to choose my next assignment. Initially, I had planned to go back to force. I wanted to leave recruiting and go back to weapons and move away from Rochester. I am not a huge fan of NY and would love not to live here. The squadron Superintendent was a career recruiter and very good at his job. He talked me into staying in recruiting and recommended me as a health professions recruiter. I would be tasked with recruiting the Air Force's Doctors and Nurses. The goal was lower for the year, and it was a pretty laid-back job. I reluctantly agreed. I immediately got a phone call from MSgt Clark, after he found out that I had put in for an assignment as a health professions recruiter. All my conversations up until this point with him had been about returning to force. He was going back into security forces and thought I was going back into weapons.

"What the hell are you doing?" He said.

"What do you mean?"

"You know what I mean. Why are you going tier 2? You hate recruiting."

"I know. The Super made it sound terrific though. So, I thought why not."

"Matt, he is a career recruiter. Did he just use PSS on you and convince you to go, or is it what you really want?"

"Crap. Son of a bitch PSS'd me."

He made me realize what I really wanted. I wanted to go back to weapons and feel like a useful part of the team again. I wanted to run a crew and mold young Airman and shape their careers. My mind was vulnerable at the time and easily influenced. I no longer knew what was best for me. Either way, I would have to move, so I might as well do something I enjoyed. I made a phone call to my First Sergeant, who was also a weapons troop and told him how I felt. Usually, it was too late to change anything, but he pulled some strings and made it happen. I got an assignment to Nellis Air Force Base in Nevada. Right outside of Las Vegas. Before I got this assignment, I had talked to Captain Barry to see if he was still stationed there. I was trying to get him to pick me up for CSAR again. He wasn't, and I'm not sure if he made any phone calls to help me out, but I did get my top choice, and that never happens to me.

I eventually went back to work as a recruiter for a few more months. Grinding it out in my office all day trying to find qualified people to join. I was not sure if I believed in the Air Force anymore. At this point, the Air Force was downsizing or "Force Shaping." It was during the Obama administration, and they were making budget cuts to our defense. I think it made us weak. Our military and country were more vulnerable than it had been in years, possibly ever. "Do more with less" was what we always heard. It meant more 12-hour shifts and weekend duty to make up for the fact that we were understaffed. The mission didn't change, just the amount of people doing it. I would be putting these kids into a situation that would be even more difficult than when I went in. I had been through a lot in the Air Force, and part of me always felt terrible that I would be putting them into harm's way. What if something bad happened to one of the kids I put in? I would feel responsible. My choice was to not put another person in the Air Force for as long as I was a recruiter. Instead, I would take care of the ones I had waiting to go and make sure they were prepared. I would hold more meetings and make sure they were both physically and mentally prepared.

There are a few recruits who always stuck out to me as being people who taught me as much as I taught them. One was John Kelley. He was a battlefield Airman. When he first came to me he wasn't even sure that he wanted to join, then he signed up and wanted security forces. I talked him into TACP. He was always up for a challenge and was probably the funniest person I ever put in. I still kept up on him after he left to make sure he was ok because his job is a hard one. He is constantly in harm's way, but it seems like he is really good at it. When he came back after his training, he would talk to my DEP and hang out with me. We went to the gym together a few times and out for drinks. We were not supposed to go out for drinks together, but if he happened to be at the same bar that I was at then, there was nothing we could do about it. I mean the town did only have one good bar.

Another Airman I put in was Sarah Hess Rossi. I took a cancellation from her. She decided not to go, then a year later asked me if she could get back in. I reluctantly let her back in and told her she would have to take any job I wanted her to do if I let her back in. She agreed. She was very irresponsible and often caused me a headache when she was in my DEP. I got her a job as a dental tech. She went into the Air Force and really excelled. She changed her ways and grew up a lot and is now a Staff Sergeant, a wife, and a great mother. I am really proud of her and all her accomplishments. It is stories like hers that made me feel good about what I was doing as a recruiter. I was giving people a chance at a better life. Ultimately it is up to the person to make the right decisions to live that life, and she was one that made the right one.

I could tell a hundred stories about the Airman that I put in the Air Force. Both good and bad. I did recruit over 100 people. That's over 100 lives that changed because they met me. 100 adventures started. 100 opportunities to improve our country. I am proud of each and every one of them. I am proud to have served beside so many great people. I wish I could give them all credit, but this is my story, not theirs, and it would be unfair of me to only talk about them a little bit when they deserve so much more.

We had found a medication that worked for me. The drug treated the symptoms but not the problem. To address the problem, I would need to talk about it. I would need therapy. My mom was pushing me to go. I was not ready. I didn't believe it would work for me because of my past experiences with it, so I refused. The medication made me almost tranquil. It took a lot of the personality out of me, but at least I wasn't angry, or mad, or having panic attacks. I still had Xanax for when they did happen but would not need it anymore. I fought back the monster and locked him in a cage. He would always try to escape, but I would not let him.

I had orders to Nellis and was supposed to report in by October. How did I go from this to a civilian in only a few short months? The hero of my story will always be a little girl named Morgan. Since she has been born, she had guided my life and led me back home. She is the reason I am alive, so naturally, it would be her that took me from SSgt Altobelli to Mr. Altobelli.

What did I learn from this part of my life? What lesson has it taught me and what can I pass on to you? If you are hurting, seek help. Don't wait. Don't try to be the strong guy or tough girl who says they don't need it because eventually you will crack, and when you do it will be ugly. I got lucky that I did not get caught the one night I went extremely nuts. I must have had someone looking out for me. It is hard to admit to yourself that you need help. It makes you feel weak and vulnerable. Sometimes the foundation you built your life on crumbles. In those moments it is necessary to hit rock bottom, so you can begin again, and create a new foundation. When you get help and genuinely commit to your health, then you will come back stronger than ever, and there is no shame in that.

Chapter 7

NECROMANCER

In the beginning of 2014, I was lying on the couch, Morgan sitting at the table, making up math problems and solving them. Not for homework, but for fun. Just because she wanted to. Most kids like to color or play games, but she wanted to learn. She ran over to me with her completed paper to show me. She asked me to check her answers and see if she got them all right. She did.

"Outstanding Morgan!" I said "I am very proud of you. When I went to your parent teacher conference the other day, your teacher said you are very advanced and doing great in school."

A smile took her face, and she was overcome with pride and acceptance, but only for a moment. Her smile quickly faded, as she looked towards the floor. She was noticeably bothered.

"What's wrong?" I asked her.

"I don't want it to be my birthday again."

"Why not? You love your birthday. You get to be whatever you want and get candy and presents. Why would you say that?" (Her birthday is on Halloween)

"Because mommy told me you are leaving, and I don't want you to go."

I looked at her face as she said that and could tell that it devastated her. I had no idea she knew I was leaving for Nellis, and I didn't even think about what it would do to her. I was too busy being mentally ill to consider what this was doing to my daughter. I paused for a moment. I had been searching for who I was, and I finally realized what that meant. I am a father. I did not want to leave my daughter so I could continue my career in the Air Force.

"Well, if that's the way you feel, then I won't go," I said to her.

"Really!?" She said as the smile returned to her face.

"I promise. I am not going anywhere."

She gave me a big hug and was happy for the rest of the weekend. I will always remember this moment as one of the best moments of my life. A moment where I am 100% sure, without a shadow of a doubt, that I made the right decision. The next day I called my squadron to tell them I wanted to deny my orders. Our manpower coordinator answered the phone and tried to talk me out of it.

"Are you sure? You know this means you will be denied re-enlistment and forced out, right?" She said.

"That is why I am doing it."

"I don't understand. Let's talk about this."

"You can talk all you want, but I am not going to change my mind on this one. I appreciate your concern, but I will be ok."

I tried to explain to her the reason I wanted to leave the Air Force, and I believe she understood because she had kids herself. My daughter was the most important thing to me. I had no plan for the future, and not even a clue of the direction to head in, but I knew this was the path I needed to be on. Not even a week later, the Air Force came out with another method to "force shape," and all those who did not have retainability would be forced out of the Air Force on May 31st, 2014. I had close to 2 months of leave saved up so now I would have only 1 month left in the Air Force, which was a dramatic switch from my plans just a week prior. I also was entitled to the Transition Assistance Program or TAPs as it was called. It was a week-long class on how to adapt to civilian life.

The class would take place on Hanscom AFB. I would need to drive back to Boston. I got approval to go and signed up for the course. The class was very informative, but if I am honest, it wasn't enough. I had no idea how to be a civilian. I still don't. I went right into the Airforce after high school, so I had no time to learn how to be an adult civilian. All my growing up took place in the Air Force. Everything is structured, and you always know exactly where you must be and when. You always know what you are supposed to be doing. The civilian world is not like that at all. You are pretty much thrown out there and told to figure it out. Everyone out there is on their own. It's dog-eat-dog. There is no team of people who have your back or can offer help if you need it like on an Air Force base.

TAPs focused on finances and getting a job. For people who wanted to start their own business, they had a course called "Boots to Business." I decided to sign up for that, but it wasn't until May. I think TAPs needs to be longer, and they need to focus more on the financial aspect and responsibilities of being a civilian, and maybe even help people get things set up. I left there and went back to Rochester. I had only another week as a recruiter before my final out processing. I would need to drive to Syracuse one more time and go over my out-processing checklist. Throughout that process I got visits from pretty much everyone in the squadron telling me I made a big mistake, and what was my plan, and blah blah blah. I don't know why they felt the need to say those things to me. The decision was made, and there was no turning back now.

When I was done in Syracuse, I drove home as a civilian. I would never put on that uniform again. I was excited and happy and felt like a tremendous weight had been lifted off my shoulders, but a great sadness overcame me at the same time. I would never put on that uniform again or be a part of something greater than myself. The pride I felt being in the Air Force would vanish and never return. I thought of my daughter and knew it was all worth it. I would make so many personal sacrifices just to see her smile. I gave up my career for her, and even now, knowing where it led me, I would do it all over again. I would suffer all the pain I have gone through and fail at all three of my business again and go bankrupt for her. When she hugs me and tells me that she loves me all my pain goes away, and I am happy. I have the sweetest little girl, and nothing can take that away from me.

Life is full of choices. Some small and some big. You make them every day. The thing is, sometimes you don't know if a decision you made is a small one or a big one until it reveals itself later. Some choices seem insignificant at the moment but could lead you to something much bigger. Every decision I have made has led me to where I am right now. Some small decisions like answering a phone call have caused me to meet people, who introduced me to other people who had a massive impact on my life. You never really know where your choices are going to lead you, and some of them might be painful, but they could lead you to something so beautiful. Something worth the pain.

Now I had a little over two months to figure my life out while I was getting paid by the Air Force. Terminal leave is a great thing. I enrolled in the National Academy of Sports Medicine to be a personal trainer. I loved training, and all my friends always asked for my advice. I got the guided study package which was a 9-week course. I then needed to pass an exam. I made it through the course while working out every day and talking about business with my gym partner. We went over our idea for the trainer tracker, an invention of ours, and he even set us up with a meeting with a large company. We met with the money guys. The decision makers and one of them was an inventor. He invented the magic eraser. We put together a presentation and worked out all the logistics of what we planned to make, and how it would work.

The presentation went well, but they wanted to see it made, and a gym use it first before funding the project. They wanted to see practical application and data. We were stuck. We thought about what we could do, and then it came to us. We could own a gym and do it ourselves. Obviously, this would take time, and we would need to build up capital. We went looking for locally owned gyms where we could train clients out of to start saving money. We checked out a bunch of different places and had no luck.

"I have one more idea," I said

"What's that?"

"Let's go to the gym I worked out at as a kid. It's a basement type, old school gym, but we might have some luck there."

"Alright, let's check it out."

We worked out a deal with the owner and began to take on clients. It was hard at first but once we had a couple, and news spread of our program we grew pretty fast. Within our first two months, we had 22 clients. We were very professional. We had professional shirts, cards, and a website. It was important that if people looked for us that they knew we were legit. We even had an LLC established. We were interested in growing our brand and getting in front of as many people as possible.

The Mr. Rochester Body Building Competition was coming up in the summer, and we thought what better way to get in front of so many like-minded people. We signed up. The federation that put on the show was the NPC (National Physique Committee). This was an untested federation, which meant that performance-enhancing drugs were allowed, and honestly even encouraged. I had never done steroids before and didn't know the first thing about them. The thing about me is when I don't understand something, I do a ton of research to find out everything there is to know about it. I am not happy until I am a subject matter expert on whatever topic it is that I am researching. I began to study the world of steroids. I wanted to give myself every advantage I could. I would sit on my computer for hours and go from website to website. Some medical, some done by bodybuilders who have used steroids. I wanted to look at it from all aspects.

Once I learned everything I felt I needed to know to make an educated decision, I just needed to find out where to get it. I now knew what I wanted to take for my goals, and how to cycle off it safely, and what amount to take for my body type and size. It was not hard to find where to get them either. It was right under my nose the whole time. I was approached in the gym one day by a man who would eventually shape a lot of my life over the next couple of years.

"Hey Matt, I heard you signed up to do the Mr. Rochester show." The man said to me.

"Yes sir, it will help bring in more clients," I answered.

"Only if you do well."

"True."

"Do you need any gear?"

"What do you mean?"

"Gear...you know. Things to help you grow brother."

"Actually yeah. I was looking."

"I have a guy. Let's not do business here though."

"Want to come over later? We can talk about it."

"Yeah, that sounds good. I got to go train my client now. Talk to you later bro." The man said as he stepped away.

Later that day he came to my house with bottles of liquid. He showed me a variety of different types of steroids. I ended up getting Testosterone E, an estrogen blocker, Clen, and HGH (human growth Hormone). The Testosterone would need to be injected directly into the muscle. At first, I hated doing this, but after a while, I got used to it. I kept my goal in mind. The estrogen blocker went under my tongue, and the HGH had to be injected around my stomach. I became obsessed with working out and getting big. I would work out in the morning and at night. Before and after my clients. I would also train abs during lunch. I wanted to win. It did not take long for me to see a difference, and this only added to my addiction to become perfect. My clients started to notice too.

How did we start our business? Well, my severance from the Air Force was close to $20,000. I also had money saved, so I had a nice little start-up fund. I bought a couple of computers, our websites, business cards, and more. I used the funds to form our LLC. I told my business partner not to worry about it, and we were 50% partners in this. This was my first business mistake, but he was a friend, and I wanted to give him his fair share since he was working on the business as hard as I was. We spent all our free time in the gym, either working out or talking to people. We became well-known in the gym. The gym owner talked us into becoming Advocare distributors to make some extra income. We had all of our clients on it. I would make a few hundred extra bucks a month off of Advocare and eventually had some of my clients become distributors. It wasn't long until I hit the adviser level. I would get 40% of all personal sales and get a 40% discount on all products. Life was good. I was making money doing something I loved. I got to work out two times a day and hang out with my friends. During this period I had forgotten all of my problems. I was actually enjoying and loving life. I was single and didn't have a girlfriend during this time, but it did not bother me. For the first time in my life, I was happy with me. I was happy by myself, and things were going great. With peaks comes valleys, and mine was about to begin.

It is my own fault really. At the time I could not see that, but now I realize what I had done. I was working hard. I took the majority of the clients and did the majority of the paperwork because my business partner had another job. He worked full time, but once we started doing well, he dropped down to part-time so he could work more hours at the gym. We had a good system where all the money went into our business account, and then we each took a percentage at the end of the month. The rate would be the same. At first, I was okay with this. To be honest, I didn't really do this for the money. I know that sounds dumb, but it's true. I did it because I loved to do it, and I was good at it. I enjoyed helping people and helping them change their lives. I even moved in with my business partner and paid him $400 a month to help with bills, since he dropped down to part-time. I figured this would help me save money as well, and we spent a lot of time together already, and he had room in the basement for me. I moved in, and it went pretty well at first. This was the second business mistake I made though.

It was soon after that people started whispering in my ear. The gym owner for one. Telling me that I was the talent and do most of the work so why am I splitting everything 50/50. I should have told them to mind their own business. Why stir the pot? The more I worked, the more I felt they were right. Then things would not be done correctly. Like he would forget to update a log or wouldn't get payment from some people. This frustrated me, and I tried to have a talk with him. My suggestion was that he let me take complete control of the company and have him as an employee until he could come in full time with me. That way I could get the business to where it needed to be without any obstacles. It sounded better in my head. This did not go over well with him. We got into an argument, and I went to my mom's.

Recently we had been given a $5000 investment. We were to use it to grow the business. I was worried that my business partner would do something irrational and I moved the money into a separate account he could not access. I would not use it, but I left it there until we decided what to do. This made him angry (as it should have. I would have been angry too) but I was worried about the business and was trying to fix it. The gym owner knew about what was going on. It's almost as if he planned it. He said they were moving locations and wanted me to run the weight room side of his fitness center. He told me to give him my business plan, and we could talk about it, but the deal only came without my business partner. This made me feel bad, but at the time it was clear that he and I were not going to see things eye to eye. I had the gym owner sign a non-disclosure agreement and gave him my business plan. I had asked for his in return so I could review it, and we could come together and make a good plan. He did not have it for me. I would ask for it over the next two weeks and try to set up a meeting, but he always seemed too busy. I am not even sure he ever had an actual business plan. In fact, it looked like he was just making things up as he went along most of the time.

He always claimed that Advocare paid him 6 figures a year, but he did not live a six-figure kind of lifestyle. I am pretty sure he was broke. He was a good talker and could convince people to do what he wanted. I realized this and then wanted nothing to do with him. I would still pay him my rent and train people there, but I didn't think I wanted to go into business with him. I don't know why I was so mad though because I was a lot like him. I would push Advocare products and tell people how great they are, and the reason I looked so good was the products, and people believed it. They would come to me to train and buy products off of me when in actuality my quick increase in muscle mass and strength was due to the steroids I was taking. I would not tell them that though. Maybe I was mad at myself just as much as I was at the Gym owner.

One day I was approached by the man who sold me the steroids and kept my secret, as he watched my business grow.

"Hey brother, what's good?" He said.

"Same old. What's up with you?"

"I wanted to talk to you about a business opportunity. Thought you might be interested."

"Oh yeah? What is it?"

"Well, I had heard you wanted to open up your own gym, and it just so happens that I found a pretty sweet location. I am looking for a partner. What do you say?"

"I will take a look at it with you. Can my business partner come?"

"Look, Matt, I like him, but I am only looking for one partner. I am not interested in splitting things three ways."

This should have been a red flag. I should have said no and stayed true to my friend. I was too ambitious for my own good, and I wanted to own a gym more than anything. I went with him to look at the location. It was filled with things from a Chinese restaurant. The owner had been using it for storage. It was a dump. The walls were moldy, and the ceiling destroyed. The roof leaked, there was no air, and it smelled terrible. It was clear that a lot of work would need to be done here. He told me to not look at it for what it was but look at it for what it could be. I had always had a good vision of what I wanted in a gym. There was a lot of open space, and two rooms. There was a bathroom and an area for an office. It could work. The rent was only $1200 a month for the location so our overhead would be low. I agreed to go into business with him. Business mistake number three, and a much bigger one. I gave him $2,000, so he could pay the down payment and get some stuff to start working.

My behavior was impulsive. Every time I made a business or life decision I had a bad feeling about it but could not help it. My demon had still been controlling me from inside his cage. My demons name was Mania. I was a maniac. I could not control myself. I had a lot of energy and focused it into blind ambition that would chip away at the very foundation of who I was.

While preparations were being made, I would still work out of the other gym and train my clients. My old business partner was still there working with me, but tensions were high. We were not getting along, and people could tell. I felt a lot of anger and resentment towards him and saw him as someone who took advantage of me and used me to start a business. That was not the case. This was my own insecurities getting in the way of progress. Who was he to me? He was a good friend. He was there for me every day. We worked out together, we went to the bar together, we talked about personal problems together. He gave me rides when I was unable to drive. He checked up on me when others left me for dead. He was a brother. I have had many brothers during my time in the Air Force, but never had a civilian turned into a brother and been someone I could trust until him. I was just too messed up at the time to realize it. My mind was destroying me from the inside out, and success was the only thing I could think about. What success meant to me was having a business that everyone knew about, and making a lot of money. To some, it might be a fulfilling life, but to me, it was a lonely one. I threw my best friend away for a chance at success.

This choice would cause me to raise the dead. My "friends" from Afghanistan would visit me in my dreams again. This only seemed to happen when I was alone. When I felt alone. I did it to myself. I wanted someone to talk to, and they were always there to listen. Never speaking, just staring, judging, and hating me. The way that I hated me. Most of these conversations happened in the mirror. I was talking to myself, but I was also talking to them. They might hate me, but I hate them just as much for making me who I was. They took a boy and turned him into a monster. They could have ignored me that night and went about their business. To be honest, I probably would have ignored them if they had. I would have made a phone call, and then went back to my RLB and went to bed. All they had to do is leave me be. Instead, the dead now walk with me and listen to my problems. Never speaking but always offering advice as to how I can hurt myself even more. The monster has freed himself from the cage.

The ability to raise the dead, to see them when I close my eyes, to be able to interact with them became a norm to me. I never could see loved ones that passed, only the people the demon wanted me to see. It was not really them. I know this. It was just a manifestation of my pain. My hatred for them, and for myself is what would guide so many of my actions through life. I was always trying to wipe away the person I was and replace him with a better, well liked, and successful individual. This was an impossible task.

At the pinnacle of my vanity was the bodybuilding competition, which took place a couple months before the events of going into business with a criminal. It took place when my old business partner and I were still brothers, and we had a common goal. It took place during a simpler time when the dead stayed dead, and my voice fell on the ears of the living.

Chapter 8

SPOT ME BRO

We were bros. The type of lunks that would get a bell rung at us in certain establishments for lifting too heavy or making too much noise. We were into every single muscle on our body and how we could define it even more. We designed intense workout programs and trained together twice a day. We had a goal in mind, and we would stop at nothing to accomplish it. We meal prepped together, we ate together, we drank protein shakes together. Consuming 3000 to 5000 calories a day. I was getting big, and strong. I was increasing at a pace that he could not keep up with, and he began to wonder why.

I knew I could trust him, so that is not why I didn't tell him I was using steroids. I didn't tell him because at the time he looked up to me, and I knew if he found out what I was doing he would want to do it too. I did not want to be a bad influence on him. Just the thought of being a bad influence should have told me that what I was doing was wrong, and I should stop, but I didn't. The shame I felt every time I went to the pharmacy to buy needles, and they would hand me a pamphlet on how to stop using drugs. I did not want to put that on him.

I was impressed with how much I could lift, and how big my muscles were becoming so I would take more. One day we were on the bench doing bench presses, and I kept loading more and more weight.

"How are you doing that?" My business partner asked.

"Doing what?"

"That! We have been training the same way, and you are getting stronger faster than me. How?"

"I don't know man. I am bigger than you, so maybe that has something to do with it. Come on. You are up."

I deflected the question and gave a vague answer. I would avoid talking about my "secret" at all costs. When clients would ask, I would tell them it was because of AdvoCare and boost my sales. Don't get me wrong. There is a lot of AdvoCare products that I like, and I do believe it helped me shed some body fat, but the muscle gain was all steroids. The man who sold me the steroids overheard our conversation and must have seen an opportunity to make another sale. When I wasn't around, he approached my business partner and told him what I was doing. Later that night, after all our clients had left, he confronted me.

"I talked to---" he said

"Oh yeah? What did he say?"

"He told me how you are getting your results. Why didn't you tell me, man?"

"I didn't want you to feel like you had to do it too. I didn't want to pressure you into anything or influence you to do them. I'm sorry. I was just looking out for you."

"Ok, that makes sense. I appreciate it."

He asked me a lot of questions about it and did his own research. He was very much like me when it came to that. He was always on his computer looking up new techniques and info on how we could do better. I can't say if he decided to take steroids or not, but he was well-informed in his decision. I was a little upset that my supplier had told him what I was doing, but I knew it was only so he could make a sale.

Every day became the same. I would get up early and meet at the gym, or we would drive together after I lived with him. We would work out before our first clients, then pound a protein shake. Train a few people and eat again. Then another protein shake. I would go into the bathroom and inject my HGH. Then we would train more people, followed by another shake and maybe some salmon or chicken. Then at night we would work out again and do some cardio and core work. We were both obsessed. My muscles grew faster, and my strength followed. Day in and day out we did the same thing. Consistency is key to results. We worked hard and sacrificed the fun we had before.

We had a little tradition that on Sundays we would go to Windjammers, a local bar, and get wings and have a couple beers. Windjammers had the best wings in town, and we always had a good time going. We had to stop for show prep. We knew it was only temporary. Being a bodybuilder takes a lot of self-control and dedication. Not everyone can do it. People look at the end result and want that type of body but don't realize what goes into getting it. It is not easy. It is not fun, and you need to be obsessed to even have a chance of making it to the stage. So many people give up only a few weeks in. They fail to stay away from that piece of cake or pizza that they really want. We didn't. We ate the same thing every day for months and stayed consistent. We stayed true to ourselves and our business.

This is where my mental disorder came in handy. I was obsessive, and ambitious and needed to be the best at what I did. Where others would fail, I would stay focused. I would not let anything come between me and my goal. This included people. If someone were not supportive of what I was doing, I would cut them out. People were expendable to me, and only success was desired.

As we got closer to the day of the show, we knew we had to learn how to hit our poses correctly. We had a pro bodybuilder that went to the gym we trained at and would talk to us from time to time. We hired him as a posing coach. I must give him credit here because he is one of the best people I have met. John Penkin is his name, and if you ever had the pleasure of watching him on stage you know, he is a man who knows his stuff. He barely charged us anything to coach us and offered up great advice all the time. He was just a really good guy who wanted to see us succeed. The more I was around the profession, the more I realized that most bodybuilders are good people. Even at the competition they are helping each other out or complementing each other. It was a close-knit family feel. Something I was familiar with, so I loved it.

Since I got out of the Airforce, I was looking for something with this feel. I was looking for a sense of belonging that I had not felt in so long. The gym is where I found it, so I made it my career and never wanted to leave. Eventually, reality would have to set in, and I would realize I could not sustain this lifestyle. Maybe if I was not a father I could have. I wouldn't need much to live, and I wouldn't have to be a role model for anyone's future. I was a father though, so I needed to think about what my actions and choices were doing to my daughter. This should have been my first priority, but I was not thinking right.

We would practice with John twice a week and then on our own every other day. We would have posing practice for an hour. Posing is an art. It is the ability to make yourself look bigger than you are in some areas and smaller than you are in others.

It is to alter the perception of your body in a favorable way so the judges will see you as the perfect person. Posing was hard. It is much harder than it looks, and by the end of it, you feel like you just worked out. We would always get sweaty and sore from posing practice. He would make us hold our poses for at least a minute so our bodies could get used to the posture. You needed to build stamina for your poses. Otherwise, you would shake while holding it, and you didn't want that up on stage. We would hold them for a long time, so when we were on stage everything looked natural and not forced.

There was so much to remember up on stage. You needed to look smooth, and have flawless transitions, and not shake, and make sure you hit the pose correctly from the judge's point of view. There were no mirrors, so you needed to go off feel. You needed to remember to smile, and stay smiling, but not look creepy while doing it. This was harder than you would think. You are thinking about everything else, the last thing you want to think about is to smile. I don't think I smiled up there. I'm not much of a smiler anyways, so I guess a smile on my face almost looks unnatural. It's not that I am always sad, or mad, I just naturally look this way. The best way to learn all of this and remember it is muscle memory. We must have gone through the poses about a thousand times each, trying to commit them to muscle memory so it would be more comfortable on the stage.

As if we didn't have enough to remember already, we each had to do a posing routine for the night show. This is where we would be called out individually and do poses to the music of our choosing. I picked the ultimate dubstep edition of sail and then edited it to what I wanted. I made it so each time the beat dropped I would transition my pose and tense up. These were not the regularly judged poses, and in fact, we could make up whatever poses we wanted. I tried to show off my strong points during my routine, focusing mainly on my arms, shoulders and broad back. I think I did pretty well. We spent hours and hours practicing our routines.

"You guys should really think about joining a natural federation. We could use some good guys like you." John Said

"That would be cool. Maybe after this show, I will." I said, knowing that I was not eligible because I had used steroids.

"I'm one of the judges for the local show. I think you both would do great in it, but you will probably get crushed in the NPC. Don't take that the wrong way. Its just you guys aren't using all the junk these guys are." John said.

I was smart about my steroid use and dosed myself slowly, so I didn't grow too big too fast. A lot of guys who use have stretch marks on their muscles. I didn't want that, so with the way, I was using steroids I avoided all of it, and it made me look natural. This was another way I was able to hide my steroid use and manipulate everyone into thinking I was doing all of this without "help."

The days leading up to the show were hectic. The final week is called peak week, and it is a challenge in itself. Your diet changes and you need to go through water manipulation to radically shrink wrap your skin to your muscles. This is a process, and there is no telling how it will turn out. I made the mistake of not doing a mock peak week before the real one to see how my body would react and what I could tweak to make it better. I was going in blind with this one.

On top of that, I needed to get rid of all my body hair and get a spray tan. Two things that, as a man, I wanted to be able to say I have never done before. It was weird, but I did it. I hated the spray tan. I had been tanning all summer and was pretty dark, but you can never be dark enough for a bodybuilding show. I had to get a spray tan, and then on top of that, we had a bronzer that we would use the day of the show. The darker you were, the more your muscles would pop, so everyone tried to be their darkest without looking too glossy. Some guys ended up looking like a golden statue. The judges hated that look. They want to know you tried, but not too hard.

A lot of people don't talk about the mental aspect of bodybuilding. The truth is, it is all mental. You need to have a sharp mind to be able to do it and survive it afterward. Here is the problem that many people face. On stage, you look your best. You have the lowest percent body fat that you have ever had before, and all your muscles are popping. People don't just walk around like this. In fact, this state is very unhealthy for your body, which needs body fat to function properly. People will begin to develop a body image problem once the show is over. They no longer look perfect, and they want to do anything to get back to that, or the opposite happens, that because they no longer look that way they give up and give in to eating unhealthy, and become obese. I have seen people suffer from anorexia and obesity because of bodybuilding. Only the mentally strong and confident can maintain a balance between the two.

I have had people come to me to train for bodybuilding shows, and the first thing I do is try to talk them out of it. I tell them how hard it's going to be and remind them of all the things they won't be able to do for so long. I inform them about the mental issues they could develop and friends they could lose because they are no longer "fun" to hang out with. I tell them that they will need to be obsessed with themselves and people will talk about it, and they are going to be judged on how they look, and they might not win. I do everything in my power to talk them out of it. If they still want to move forward with it after that, then I will train them. They must agree to listen to everything I say, and never cheat.

When people see bodybuilders, they think it's just a guy who lifts stuff and eats chicken. That is the stereotype. It is a common misconception. Some establishments perpetuate these stereotypes with their ads and "lunk alarm." Which is something I have a massive problem with. They claim to be a judgment-free zone unless you know what you are doing in the gym, in which case, they will judge you and ring an alarm to single you out. It's like high school all over again for some people, and that kind of discrimination has no place in the gym. I would never set foot in a "gym" that has purple and yellow equipment to work out anyways.

What a bodybuilder really does is carefully calculates the number of nutrients their body needs to perform at its maximum potential. This means balancing all your foods and using a food scale to make sure you are hitting the right number of protein, carbs, and fats. There is a science to it. Then there is something called carb cycling where you trick your body into releasing glycogen storage by spiking your carbs one day and dropping them the next. These have some adverse effects on your metabolism if you continue to do them for any length of time, so it is important to stop when you aren't prepping for a show.

On top of that, they need to look at their body as a symmetrical piece of clay. Each side must match the other, so you need to design your workouts around your flaws, so when you hit the stage, you appear to be flawless. A lot of hard work and dedication goes into the sport, and I have a lot of respect for anyone that decides to take on the challenge.

The day of the competition was nerve-racking. I woke up early and grabbed everything I would need for the show. I had it all packed the night before. We had to be at the convention center by 7. We waited outside the doors until they were ready for us to come in and complete registration. Since I had never competed before, I had to register with the NPC. It cost about $100, but I would get a subscription to the magazine and be able to compete in any NPC show for a year. We went over and verified what class we would be competing in. I was in three categories. I did Men's physique, which I did just for fun because I am too big for that class, and Bodybuilding Novice and Bodybuilding Open. I was in the light heavyweight class. I weighed in at 196lbs.

They lined us up and gave us numbers. Then they went over how the show will work. They went over when each class would take the stage and what poses the judges would call out. They introduced the judges and then showed us where we could get ready. Men and women were separated backstage. Men took the left side of the stage and women had the right. In the middle was a little workout room where you could try to keep your pump for the stage. There are all sorts of tricks people used to make themselves look pumped up on stage. Some eat a piece of dark chocolate before going on stage to make their veins pop out. Some drink a shot of wine, which has the same effect. I went with the small chocolate piece. I did not eat much that day and only sipped water as needed. You didn't want your body to look smooth. You wanted a muscular and vascular look. Basically, you had to expel as much water from your body as possible. This made the stage more difficult. Lack of food and water doesn't help you remember your poses.

The smell of tanning oil and lotion filled the Air. The men's and woman's side were separated by a curtain. Our first category would be Men's Physique. We would wear board shorts and only have to hit a few poses. This category picks the person who would look good on a beach. You don't need to be crazy huge, in fact, it's judged against you if you are. You want a nice V shape to your upper body with a little definition. My shorts were in the pattern of the American flag. This was a mistake. It took away attention from my body. It was too busy, and it cost me some points. I should have gone with all black, or all blue. I wanted to stand out, and I did, just not for the right reason. That's what being a real American is all about I suppose. We would walk out one by one and smile, do our couple poses and come back. It was mindless and easy. It isn't my favorite category. There is minimal skill involved. The bodybuilding classes require many more poses and the ability to choreograph your own routine. It is more of a challenge, and I had more fun doing it.

It would be a couple hours before I retook the stage for the bodybuilding class. Most of the day is just waiting around for your turn. You are on stage a total of three minutes but are there from 7am until 10pm. It's funny when you think about it. Months of hard work and dedication, all the food you had to prep and eat, all the workouts you had to do, all the cardio you suffered through, all for three minutes on stage. Is it worth it? That is for you to decide. For me, it was worth it. It was something I wanted to do, and it is something I am proud of. While waiting, I went out into the crowd and talked to my friends and family who were there to support me.

"You look hot!" Said my friend Lisa in support.

"Thanks, I appreciate that," I said as I chuckled from her comment.

"When do you go on again?" Said my friend Amanda

"Not for a little while, so I am going to sit out here and watch the other competitors," I said.

It is funny how damaging a simple compliment can be to someone who has a mental disorder. "You look hot." Those three words are all it took for me to develop a complex. It was meant to be supportive, and at the moment it was, but what I really heard was, "When you don't look like this you are not as good-looking."

This would be the beginning of me being hard on myself about how I looked. I knew in my head that it was impossible to walk around lean all the time, and even unhealthy, but If I gained even a little fat, I would overly criticize myself.

It must have been funny for my high school friends to see. In high school, I was a tiny kid. I did not have much muscle mass and did not really put on any size until a couple years into my enlistment in the Air Force. To them, I was a completely different person. That was basically true. I was not that kid anymore. Barely any part of that kid had survived everything I had been through up to this point. Even as I think back on my days in high school, it is as if I remember someone else. It doesn't even feel like I lived those days. There are parts of my past that I can't remember. It's as if I was born again once I went to war, and my history was erased. That was just some kid I had heard of, seen some pictures or movies of, but it was not me.

It was almost time for me to retake the stage, so I headed back to the weight room and got a quick pump in. As I looked at my competition, it was clear that I was not going to take first. I thought I could take second though. I knew first would go to this guy who was absolutely gigantic, and looked like he didn't have an ounce of body fat on him. I knew he would beat me. He showed up leaner and more cut than me. I was competing against a couple other guys in my class as well. I had a bigger upper body, and my arms were massive. I knew if I hit my poses right I could probably beat them. That was my goal. Second place still qualified in these shows, so I wanted to get second. I had trained hard and ate clean for a long time. I wanted this victory.

We all took the stage and hit our first pose. "Quarter turn to the right" the judges would say, and we would hit our next pose. They ran through each pose twice, making us hold it for at least 30 seconds as they compared us. They called out a couple numbers and made us switch places, so they could see a side by side comparison of two people they thought were close. I got called and moved towards the middle. There are little tricks to learn if you get called. You want to step out in front of the other person who was called, so the judges stayed focused on you, and it displays confidence. When both competitors know this, it becomes a game of chicken. I backed down and stepped to the right, letting the other guy pass in front of me. To me, it was better than running right into him and looking awkward. It didn't appear as though he would move. Once set up again, they called out all the positions. We hit quarter turn after quarter turn. I would exhale all the air in my lungs and tense up trying to make every muscle in my body pop out. I would hold it for as long as I could and try to remember not to shake. It took a lot of control. The lights were directly on us. They were bright and hot. We all were sweating. It was a combination of the heat, the poses, and nerves. Finally, we heard the judges say, "Thank you, please step off-stage." We exited the stage and now had a break before the night show.

The show is broken into two parts. There is prejudging which happens in the morning and usually finished by 1 or 2pm. Then the night show which began at 6pm. We had to be back at 5. There was not much we could do though. Usually, people would go and eat sushi or a burger with only half the bun to get some carbs in them and make their muscles look fuller for the night show. The competition is won or lost during prejudging. The judges usually know who they are going to pick as the winners by the end of the morning. The night show is just for fun, and for the audience to enjoy the show. This is where we would do our routines to music. Sometimes, if the competition is close, then the night show can make a difference in who wins. You never know, so you always go out and give it your best.

They call out the groups for the night show the same way they did during prejudging. It was like reliving the morning all over again, only this time it would be longer because instead of calling all of us out for bodybuilding at once, they would call us out one by one, so we could do our routine. The routines lasted between 60 and 120 seconds. I had a few other people I knew in the competition and would watch their routines and cheer them on.

My turn to take the stage. My music began to play, and I walked out to my spot in the center stage. I wanted to start with my strength. I had my back turned to the audience and the judges. The first beat dropped, and I hit a rear double bicep pose from a lat spread, so my back stayed looking big. I would then turn and hit a side tricep pose until finally I would face front and hit a front double bicep pose. I started with all upper body and then moved down my body with the poses. I went to a chest pose, then abs and legs. I had practiced this routine hundreds of times, and it paid off because I did not forget a single pose or miss a beat. I waved at the end of it, and walked off-stage, chest puffed out and head held high. It was out of my hands now. It was up to the judges.

My friend Julie was there with an AdvoCare table set up. I walked over to her booth, and she had some re-hydrate ready for me.

"Good job Matt. Here take this." She said as she handed me the drink.

"Thank you so much. You saved me! I was starting to get dizzy." I said as I slammed the drink like a shot.

I watched the rest of the show with my friends and family in the audience until I had to go back for the awards. They all told me I did well, and they were proud of me. I was excited to be done and looking forward to going out after and eating. That's all

I could think about at the time was how hungry I was and how I couldn't wait to eat. We had planned to go to Windjammers after the show to get some wings and drinks. As supportive as I was of everyone else competing, I kind of didn't care to watch them anymore. I had been there all day and was ready for it to be over. Finally, the time came for the awards. Just like prejudging and the night show, the awards were given by class in the same order, and then at the end, they would crown Mr. and Mrs. Rochester. I had no shot at that. At least not this time around. Maybe one day, I thought to myself.

They called my group out. I stood there waiting for the results. They call them from last to first. I already knew who was going to take first, so I was hoping not to hear my name until they got to second place. Unfortunately, they called my name for third, which isn't placing. I was a little disappointed, but also happy and relieved that it was over. I took home that trophy and 4th place for Men's Physique, which I think I threw away because I didn't care about it at all. I stayed until the end when they decided who won overall and got the title, Mr. Rochester. It was the biggest guy in the show. I had him picked for it all along and was just happy I wasn't competing against him.

We got dressed and headed for Windjammers with all our friends. I was meeting a girl there that I had been talking to and invited a girl that worked at the gym, who I knew liked me. I can't say for sure why I did it, because the girl that was into me left abruptly, without saying bye, and was very mad at me. Honestly, I didn't care about either girl at the time. I was hungry and wanted food! Sweet Canadian and Smokey Mountain with harbor fries was always my order there. They are the best wings and fries in town. It was a Saturday night, so the bar was packed. We ordered drinks too, and those came out first. I was two beers deep before my food came out. Two beers on an empty stomach with almost no water all day. I figured I was going to get drunk that night, and I did. We ate and had a good time. The funny thing about depriving yourself of all the good tasting food for so long is when you can finally have it you want it all. We gave ourselves two days to eat whatever we wanted.

The next morning, I woke up and had a whole package of Oreo's for breakfast. Not a sleeve, the entire thing. We ordered a pizza for lunch and ate all of it. I am pretty sure we went back to Windjammers for dinner since it was Sunday and we could do our Sunday tradition again. So much good food. We ate ice cream again and drank beer, and enjoyed a little bit of the summer before going back to being strict. We had planned to do the show in October as well, so we didn't want to let ourselves go too far. We had plans for so much. We were good friends, and we should have been able to work together and achieve all our business goals, but my ambition got in the way, and I had people whispering in my ear. It would soon all fall apart. It fell apart, and I became a gym owner.

Business has cost more than just time and money. It is a strain on relationships. It can crush longtime friendships. It takes a particular type of person to own a business. Successful businessmen are narcissistic, obsessive, and usually a bit greedy. These are qualities that I do not possess. I always tried to do business honestly and ethically. I would report all my income on my taxes, and give people a reasonable price for services, much better than my competition, and believed if I took care of enough people, then the people, or maybe the universe would take care of me. This is a nice sentiment that is usually lost in reality.

We do not live in a book or movie world. Not everyone gets a happy ending, which is why sometimes I hate the saying that everything happens for a reason. It is something that I try to believe, but in the end, I go right back to Afghanistan and realize that the children dying from war, or starvation died for nothing. There was no bigger plan for them. They would not believe that their death led to something better. In the grand scheme of things sometimes bad things happen because bad things happen. There is no rhyme or reason for it. Sometimes I wonder if I get a happy ending or if my life will just end in tragedy. It is a nice way to think, that the pain you are going thru is for some higher purpose, and often I tell myself that too, but a part of me can't help but think about the people that never had a chance and wonder, what was it all for.

Another saying I really hate is when all these entrepreneurial types say, "No risk, no reward." A philosophy I lived by for a long time. What they don't tell you is what happens when you take the risk, and it doesn't work out. When you fail. All the pain and suffering you will go through when you lose everything. Then you see people who tell you that you need to fail multiple times to succeed. I have become pretty experienced in failing and keep taking risks and feel no closer to the success promised by the business gurus.

The very last thing that happened with our business was a meeting with a Welcome Wagon representative. They would design an ad for us and deliver it to every new homeowner in the local area, and we would get a contact list of everyone who was new, so we could call them and offer them a welcome deal. This was an expensive service, but if we acted during the meeting, they were going to knock a significant amount of money off the price. This was a sales tactic that I have used, so I knew what they were doing, but I still wanted it. My business partner looked at the saleswoman and said, "We are not in the position today to make a decision." I did not want the opportunity to pass by, so after she left, and he left, I called her to explain what was going on with the business. She came back to the gym to talk to me again. She basically talked me into going off on my own and getting in before any of my competition. I did. I applied for a new LLC and bought a new website and signed up with Welcome Wagon. Within a matter of hours "Swoll fitness" was born. I know it's a dumb name, but I was put on the spot and couldn't think of anything else.

I went back to the house where I had been living to tell him that I was going off on my own.

"Hey. I called the Welcome Wagon lady back and took her offer. I made my own business and am going off on my own."

"Ok." He said

"Also, I am going to go and stay with my mom."

"What happened to us, Matt? We were brothers."

"I'm sorry, but after everything, I just can't trust you."

I left his house, and this would regrettably be the last conversation we would have. I lost a friend, and a brother that day all because I wanted to improve the business. I chose the company and money over a person who had my back time and time again, and I hated myself for it. I couldn't see how messed up it was at the time though. I had no impulse control and did what I thought had to be done.

My finances had taken a hit with starting two new business so closely together. They were about to take another hit. As I said before, the owner of the gym I trained at had asked me to run the weight room of his new location. I had given the owner my business plan and got nothing in return. We scheduled a meeting, and he kept rescheduling because he wasn't ready to move forward. I began to get impatient and when approached by the other trainer who wanted to open a gym, decided to take a look. I did not see the harm in looking.

I met him at a location in Henrietta. The place was behind a building but on a busy intersection. The building could be seen from 3 of the 4 roads on the intersection, so it did have some value there. We walked inside and found a mess. As I said before, it was storage for a chain of Chinese restaurants. It was about 2000 square feet and mostly open space, perfect for a small personal training studio. It needed to have a lot of work done, but I could see the potential in it. I think that the timing of the opportunity had a lot to do with my decision to move forward. If it had been any earlier, I would have said no because my business was doing well, and so were we. If it were any later after I had recovered from the loss or decided to move forward with the other gym, I would have said no. I was in the middle of businesses and had no idea what I was going to do, which made it easy to say yes.

The man I decided to go into business with was huge and strong. He knew what he was doing when it came to the weight room, but I believe most of his size could be attributed to the use of steroids. I am not one to talk, because I used them to get bigger too, just not as big as him. He was an excellent speaker when it came to people. He knew how to get people on his side and was very charismatic. He was the person I described earlier and anyone who stood in his way he would get rid of one way or another. He was also a hot head, who let his temper get the best of him on many occasions. His past was the opposite of mine. I spent 8 years in the Air Force, and he spent 8 years in prison. He had five felonies. He basically got them all in the same day. I am not exactly sure what they were, but all I know is he did some bad things for some bad people. So why go into business with him? A sane person with a working brain would not have, but my vision was skewed by ambition and my own past. I needed to be someone, and I wanted to own this gym. He did have his good qualities. He was a deal maker and usually got us good prices on stuff and was not afraid to push people when need be.

He is the reason for the saying "Nice guys finish last." I find this saying to be pretty accurate. They finish last because of people like my new business partner, who is willing to do anything for success, no matter how illegal or immoral. A person like that will do things that a nice guy will not, and therefore it is tough for a nice guy to come out ahead. It is not that the system is rigged against him. It is that he will stay inside the system, while others work outside of it.

Chapter 9

BUILDING ROME

We made a deal with the landlord and got 4 months free while we cleaned out the location and set up the gym. We needed all the time we could get. The first task was getting all the junk out of there. This took a day. Us and a couple of friends opened the doors and got to work. We had a dumpster brought to the location and threw away anything the owner did not want. At the end of the day, the place was completely empty but still a mess. Holes covered the walls and ceiling. A lot of electrical work needed to be done as well. We put a lot of sweat equity into the building doing most of the work ourselves. We killed all the mold ourselves. We painted the whole inside, and outside ourselves. We built walls ourselves. We put in flooring ourselves. Day in and day out I would spend 12 to 14 hours in that place working on getting it perfect. I put a lot of time, and the rest of the money I had into that place. It was my baby. (Thanks Mania!)

My business partner and I got along the whole time we were working on the gym. It was actually a lot of fun, and I had a good feeling about this business. I had made a pretty solid business plan and altered it to our new location. I knew we needed to be different, so that is what I planned to do. We had projected 40 members for pre-sales. While I was working on this project, I lost all my clients. I didn't so much lose them, as I had to put them on hold. I was forced to do this because I no longer had a place to train them.

I had scheduled a meeting with the gym owner of the gym I trained out of and his girlfriend. They co-owned the gym, but I found out later that it was mostly her. My new business partner and I sat with them to explain we were opening up our own spot and if their gym flooded again (which it often did), they could come to use our facility.

"You guys wanted to talk to us?" Said the gym owner.

"Yes, I just wanted to let you know that we have decided to open up a gym in Henrietta. We have been working on it and thought you should know." I answered.

"Well, that's really dumb." He responded in anger. "We had plans to go into our new gym together. You are bailing on us?"

"I asked to see your business plan for over a month, and you never gave it to me, while you had mine. It didn't seem like we were moving forward, and I needed to do something. Besides, when I first came to you, I told you that my goal was to own a gym in a year."

"No, this is not ok. You are competition now!"

"How? We are in a completely different town, and no one is going to drive 20 minutes to come to our gym from here."

"I don't care. This meeting is over." He said as he got up and left.

It was clear that I had worn out my welcome there, so I left and did not return. Our working relationship was over, which caused me to not want to take part in AdvoCare anymore. I no longer wanted to make him money, so I stopped doing it. A bad move on my part, because I also stopped making money myself, and I now know that I bit my nose to spite my face.

I had no backup plan. I had no way to make money now, so I needed to make sure this worked. I went a long time without making any money and resorted to credit. It was a bad idea and eventually ended up hurting me. I did not anticipate failing, as most people don't. I thought I would make money and pay it all back. I was all in, and I wanted this to work more than anything. We started working on location in July, and we finished in October. Even though I worked a lot and was stressed out, and had no money left, it was a lot of fun. We had a good time building it up to be as perfect as it was. We also got lucky a few times. There was a CrossFit gym that went out of business, and we ended up buying all their equipment for only $7,000. He wanted more but was not in a position to negotiate because he needed the money. That is what my business partner was good at. Finding an opportunity and exploiting it. I was a fool to think he wouldn't do the same thing to me.

The equipment we got from the CrossFit gym was excellent, but it was not enough, so we had to order some new stuff online, and pick up a few other pieces around town. One of the pieces we ordered was a dual adjustable cable machine. We put together all the equipment ourselves and saved this one for last. It was by far the most difficult one to put together. Our grand opening would be the next day, and I needed to get it done. I stayed until 3am to make sure it was done. I spent hours trying to make sure it worked properly so if anyone wanted to try it during the opening they could. The grand opening would be our chance to show off all the work we put in and inspire people to want to work out in our gym. It took us a lot of work to even get people to come. We pounded the pavement going from business to business handing out fliers and free memberships to business owners in hopes that they would bring their employees. I was a member of the Greece Chamber of Commerce and talked to them to set up a ribbon cutting ceremony and even got a local politician to come make an appearance. The local paper covered the opening, and it was on the front page of the Henrietta post. I believe the grand opening was a huge success. We had over 100 new leads to call and try to set up consultations for training.

Things seemed to be going well. We had staff trainers to help drive in new business, and we had our own clients. I used a software that helped us track and manage our members and staff, and spent hours loading all our guests from the grand opening and setting follow-ups. I made the training schedule, and goals for the trainers. I also created and managed the website. I did a lot of the work behind the scenes to make sure everything would run smooth. My business partner was constantly on the phone with new people, schools, and sports teams to try to get us new contracts. We ended up landing a deal with a local hockey team. They would use our facility two times a week and pay us $400 a month. Things were looking up. I had staff meetings to train people on the system we used and made sure that they were using it.

Where did it all go wrong? A couple places actually. The first reason that the business failed is the way we structured it. We had to put a loan against the LLC for the amount of the equipment since I ran out of money. The money came from my business partner who would take all profits until the loan was repaid. This meant that I could not take any draws but could make money off my personal training clients. At first, I was okay with this, but it became a problem. He was training people all day, and I needed to spend time with the back-office responsibilities; things that I would not get paid for, which left little time to train clients. Managing the business was very time-consuming. I trained a few clients when I had time but could not devote the time needed to build up a large enough clientele to make enough money to pay my bills. I went to my business partner and purposed a solution.

"Hey man, can we talk?" I said.

"Yeah, what's up?"

"I am just having a hard time paying my bills or finding the time to train more clients. I have to manage the website, and schedule, and trainers, and our gyms software, and it's time-consuming, and I don't get paid for it."

"Well, do we really need all that stuff?" He asked.

"Yeah, it keeps us organized and professional and allows people to book stuff online. It is important."

"Ok, I just don't think we need it. So, what do you want me to do? We need to pay back the loan against the LLC."

"I know. Here is my idea. You keep all the business revenue, all the memberships, everything that comes through the LLC. We pool our Personal Training money, and both take draws off that. It is like what they do in law offices when there is a partnership. This way we both make money, and we aren't in competition with each other for clients, because that doesn't make sense."

"No," He said as he turned red and stood up. "I am sick of you talking to my clients and using my gym. All of this is mine, and I will do whatever I want with it!" He now grabbed me by the shirt and had his fist up like he was going to hit me.

"What are you doing!? Let go of me!" I yelled at him

I had my knife in my pocket and put my hand in there ready to pull it out if he hit me. He was much bigger than I, and I knew a hit from him would disorient me, and I would not be able to fight him off without a weapon. He let go of me, screamed, threw his chair, and left. He was outside, on the phone pacing back and forth. He knew he allowed his temper to get the best of him and it probably wasn't a good move, especially for someone on probation. I am sure he was on the phone with his father, who would bail him out of any bad situation he was in now. I did not stick around to see what would happen next. I left and went back home.

The drive home toyed with my mind. I am not sure how I even ended up getting home, because the only thing I could see was an image of my knife plunged into his neck. I would run through the scenario, where I gave him no time to let go of me, and instead reacted as I knew how. The picture of him bleeding out on the ground brought back familiar feelings from a time long ago. I knew the likelihood of me getting away with it was high. An Air Force veteran acting in self-defense against a guy who was two times my size with violent felony convictions. No one would question me. I also knew that if I had done that, I probably would not recover. I needed my sanity more than I needed my safety.

I no longer knew what to do. I was not making money personally, and my business partner had pushed me out of all decision-making. He took my plan and changed it. Instead of having staff trainers he made them pay us to use the gym and have their own clients. I don't like this strategy in a gym because it promotes competition, and usually leads to fights and problems, not people working together towards a common goal. It also caps the amount of revenue the gym would be able to make. He got rid of payroll and the systems I used to track clients and employees and started to operate off the books. The business was no longer in legal compliant status, and I no longer wanted anything to do with it. Why all the changes? We didn't hit our forecasted number of pre-sales. We had about 20, but we had over 100 leads. I tried to explain that sometimes things don't go as planned, but we needed to stay consistent if we wanted to succeed. Instead, he went back to a system we had seen fail from the previous gym we worked at. It wasn't smart. It doesn't work.

Now I would sink into a more profound depression. I would go to work and fear for my safety and know that if I said anything my business partner didn't agree with he would just blow up on me. I was working there for free and made no money. I had put everything I had into this, and I didn't want to lose it, so I held on for as long as I could. My finances suffered, so I put my resume online and started looking for a job I could do part-time. I instantly got a lot of phone calls and set up about 8 interviews. I wanted the gym to be my main focus but do something on the side to have a guaranteed paycheck. Originally that was the plan, but eventually, I realized that I could not succeed in the same space with my business partner and asked him to buy me out, he decided that he did not want to do that. I tried to buy him out, and he said no to that as well. I was stuck in the LLC until I had some leverage, which eventually I got.

I knew what this meant for me. It meant starting all over again. No money, no home, and behind on my car payments. This had to be rock bottom for me. I thought I hit it before, but I was wrong. This was it, I thought. I would end up being wrong about that too. My sickness had not finished with me and would build me back up a couple more times only to lose everything again.

I went back to what I knew. Everything I applied for had something to do with recruiting or sales, which I was very good at. I knew that I could make some money doing it. I went on two interviews. The first one was with Primerica Financial Services, which if you have never heard of, is the network marketing craze of the financial world. I did not know this at the time. I interviewed, and they really liked me. Usually, if you want to be a part of it, you have to pay a fee to take the class and sign up. I did not have to pay. The office covered it for me and didn't even tell me there was a fee, so they must have liked me or saw potential. The other interview I went on was for Interim Healthcare as an HR manager. I got that job as well but would not start it until December. Their goal for me was to build up another office in Canandaigua and eventually run it. It was a company I could have had a future with if I was smart and decided to stay. Again, I let my ambition get the best of me.

I now had two new jobs and would put the gym on hold. I hoped that my absence would be noticed, and my business partner would want me to come back and work out a deal, so I could actually get paid something. He was too proud for that though. Even if he thought it, he never would have told me. I told him that I needed some time off to focus on building my bank account back up. He was understanding and said he had everything under control. I took one last look around the gym that I had put so much of my time in and said goodbye. It was sad and caused me great pain to leave it. I felt like I was giving up my dream.

I would like to tell you that I learned to be smarter with my business decisions in the future. I would love for this to be the last big mistake that I made, but unfortunately, I cannot say that. I should have learned a lot of valuable lessons from this experience, and perhaps I did, but I would not realize it until much later. I was still under the impression that I did everything right and was forced out of my own business, but mistakes were made by me that I was not ready to admit.

Chapter 10

NOW HIRING
HEARTBEATS

Interim Healthcare was short-lived, and Primerica would end up being the reason why I left. My plan of action for these two jobs was I would work at Interim from 8am until 5 or 6pm Monday thru Friday, and after work, I would go hold one or two appointments for Primerica. I would work a lot of hours, but I was used to it so I wouldn't mind. The only days I would make sure not to work in the evening was Thursday so I could see Morgan.

The interview process was not bad at all. I first spoke on the phone with the head of HR for the whole company. Then she set up a face to face meeting with the Head of the office, and the HR manager for Rochester, so I could interview with them, and they could see if I would be a good fit for the office. I showed up to the office 15 minutes early, which was normal for me thanks to the military. I sat in the waiting room, and apparently, they were dealing with some issues that day (which later I found out was a typical day) because they didn't start my interview until a half hour after it was scheduled. I waited patiently though as I really wanted the job. Finally, I was called back into the office.

I met with the administrator who ran the office and the HR Manager. They were both so friendly and seemed happy to see me. They asked me questions about my past, and why I wanted the job and why I would be good at it. I talked to them about my recruiting days and owning a business. Since I would be tasked with starting up a whole new office, I thought it was important to tell them about that. They loved me and recommended me to the head of HR who then called me back to discuss my contract. I got to negotiate my pay. I was not very smart when it came to this and settled at $17 an hour. I know that it may seem like a lot to some people, but I was getting paid 40 or 50 an hour as a personal trainer, and as a financial planner sometimes I made 500 to 800 in an hour. I got spoiled with high standards, and I think if I negotiated a higher contract I might have stayed with them.

They gave me a start date for the beginning of December. This gave me time to build up my financial business before starting my full-time job. I treated Primerica like a full-time job. I would go into the office at 8 or 9 every day and make phone calls or learn something new until I was very good at it. Once I did start working at Interim I actually really enjoyed it, for a little while. I would go in, and everyone was so friendly to me and respected me because of my position. Most of the job was paperwork and administrative when you weren't holding interviews or searching for new Home Health Aids, or Nurses. I would post on Job sites, and answer e-mails and set up new meetings. I would hold interviews and get their file ready to go for hiring.

Hiring for a healthcare company was nothing like recruiting for the Air Force. These people came to me and wanted the job.

I never had to talk anyone into taking a position. If they were qualified, I would hire them. It was that simple. I loved giving people jobs and felt like I was helping. I would be staffing for people who needed care, and it was my job to hire people who would care for them. I loved it. There was also a dark side to the position though. I had to fire people. Unfortunately, people don't always do the right thing, and a lot of times they would get caught. It was my job to talk to them about the events that took place. Depending on the severity of their actions I would have to assign a consequence. Sometimes it was just a write-up so we could keep it on file that they have been warned. Sometimes it was a final warning, and anything else from this point forward would result in termination. In cases of theft, it was automatic termination. We had some people do some really desperate things.

People would get caught on a nanny cam stealing and then deny to us that they did it until we told them that we had the video. Then when I went to fire them, they would give me a sob story about how they can't pay their bills, and I was ruining their kids Christmas. They tried to make me feel bad. We all go through hard times, and I understand that, but if I didn't fire them, I could have lost my job. It was the ugly side of my job, and near the holidays it seemed to be worse. It seemed like I was firing more people than we were hiring. This ended up weighing on me profoundly and motivated my decision to leave. I liked improving people's lives, and sometimes I felt like I was hurting people, even though it was their own fault, I just didn't like being involved in the process.

The people that worked in the office were very friendly, and we all usually had a good time. Every day was filled with laughs and jokes. The company did an excellent job at rewarding its people. This office was very profitable for the company, so the owner took everyone to Paris. Apparently, because I was new, I did not get to go. Someone had to stay behind and work. I met the owner a couple times, and he was a very nice older gentleman. He told me he heard good things about me and had plans for me. I should have seen all the signs that this company was grooming me to be something bigger than an HR manager, but I was blind. I wanted to be successful so bad that I threw away good opportunities for success. It doesn't make sense, I know, but my brain wasn't working all that well at the time.

So here is the part where I tell you the reason for all of it. I only worked at Interim Healthcare for three months, so why was that a part of my life? How does this fit in as it pertains to the bigger picture? If you are one of those "everything happens for a reason" people, then here it is. In the middle of December, I got a message from a girl named Amanda. She told me that she knew someone that I trained at my gym, and he told her to message me because she is a nurse and looking for a job. I was very professional and gave her my email address to email me her resume and I would set up an interview. She emailed me her resume, and it was very impressive. I emailed her back to set up a meeting. We set a date for the following week. The day before the meeting she sent me a text and said that she could not make it in. She said she was going through a lot, and she would call me when she was ready for the interview. I told her that I understood (even though I didn't) and to let me know when she was ready.

I expected that to be the last I ever heard from her, but the following week she sent me a text and asked to set up another interview. I did for a couple days later. She didn't show and sent me a text after apologizing and said that she wasn't ready for this yet. I said ok, and to let me know when she was ready. I thought this would definitely be the last time I would ever hear from her, and on a professional level, it was. The next time I heard from her was New Year's Eve. I was sitting at home, because I had nothing to do, and decided that I should no longer go out on New Year's Eve anyway. I received a text from Amanda that said "Happy New Year Matt. I appreciate you." I had not done much for her, so I don't know why she said she appreciated me, but I liked to be appreciated, so I text her back "Happy New Year." I kept thinking about her text, and I was sitting in bed alone, so I decided to text her again. I asked her what was going on, and if she was alright. She had said she had a lot going on in her life, and couldn't commit to the job. I wanted to talk about it. I found out that she had an 8-month-old baby boy, who was born prematurely. Her ex-boyfriend had kicked her out of the house because he was "no longer attracted to her" and she had to move back in with her parents. She was depressed. A feeling I knew all too well. I talked about my past experiences, and we spoke on the phone for a few hours. Connecting with someone on that level was nice.

I did not know her well, and I had only seen her picture on Facebook, but I enjoyed talking to her and thought she was a wonderful person, so I asked her to go to a movie with me. She said yes. Part of me was worried because she was just out of her last relationship, and I was in no way wanting to be a rebound. On the third of January, we went to the movies to see "Horrible Bosses 2". I offered to pick her up, but she said she would drive and meet me there. She was surprised I even offered to pick her up. I found that sad. Guys don't do that anymore I guess.

I wore an argyle sweater and jeans. I made sure my hair looked nice and wanted to look my best to impress her. I walked in and instantly saw her standing there. She had bright golden blonde hair and looked at me and smiled. I felt butterflies instantly. I was speechless. Like I really don't remember if I said anything. I know I wanted to talk to her, but I had never met a woman as beautiful as her before. The rest of the date I would just try to not make a fool out of myself. The funny thing is, she admitted to me later that she felt the same way and was trying not to make a fool out of herself.

We watched the movie and laughed. I held her hand for a minute, but then she pulled away because she said her palms were sweaty. I didn't care. Mine probably was too. I was so nervous. After the movie, we walked outside to my car. She asked me if I wanted to go to Tim Horton's for hot chocolate. I said yes. She said she would pay since I got the movie. I wouldn't have let her pay anyways, but we got half-way there, and she realized she left her purse in the movie theater. We went through the drive-thru and got our hot chocolate, and I raced back to the theater to see if her purse was still there. It was. She got lucky. We sat in my car sipping hot chocolate and talked for about two hours. We shared everything. She was so easy for me to open up to, and she opened up to me. I really liked her. It was getting late, and she needed to get home, so I said goodbye and drove home.

Once I got back, I sent her a text and told her to text me when she got home, and that I'd had a lot of fun and wanted to see her again. She wanted to see me too. This is how our relationship started. Interim Healthcare was how we met, and for that, I am happy that I took that job. It was the reason I met my future wife and the love of my life. She is everything I have ever wanted in a woman and a fantastic role model for my daughter. When times are tough, I just have to look at her and remind myself how lucky I am to have someone who loves me as much as she does.

How did I leave Interim healthcare? It was February. I was starting to pick up steam on my financial business with Primerica. The head of HR for the company was in our office for a few days to go over stuff with me and see how things were going with the new office set up. The new office was going to be a challenge. It was in a small storage facility building, and almost impossible to find if you didn't already know where it was. The next problem was there is no room for growth in that building. It had one office in it for us. If we were going to grow, we would need a bigger office so we could put some schedulers in there. Then I had to make sure I had enough people to staff the jobs we had down there. We took on a new contract before we had the people to fill it, so this was a headache. We would get people from Rochester to drive down to Canandaigua to fill these jobs and end up paying them more to do it. Already off to a bad start. Even with all the challenges the new office did make the company an extra $9,000 a week. If I knew anything about healthcare or how to start up a healthcare company, I think that is what I would do next. It is profitable, and always in demand. There is a lot to it though, and I know nothing of the business side, so I would never even try that.

The job was demanding, and a lot of driving for me. The pay was not really worth it. The night before I put my 2 weeks in I had made a sale in my financial business and made a little over $1,000. I was thinking to myself that's more than I make in a whole pay period with this job. If I focus on my financial business, I would be able to grow it and make some excellent money. Plus, I was still helping people. Just with their finances and securing a future for their families. This swayed my decision. I told the head of HR what was going on, and how I needed to focus on my other business because I had a future there. She told me that I had a future with them as well. I knew that and should have taken it seriously, but my brain would not let me. Who knows where I would be right now if I had. I insisted though that I needed to do this right now. I gave her my two weeks, and she was very understanding about it. She was not mad and didn't make me feel bad for my decision. I have a lot of respect for the people of that company and everything that they do.

On Saturday I went into the Primerica office. We did training every Saturday morning. I led a few of them already because I was a good recruiter and build a team quickly. Our Regional Vice Presidents had won a trip to Puerto Rico from the company. Every six months Primerica gives another trip to their top producers in each category. They were going to call me from there, during training so he could talk to the base shop. I told him that I quit my job and would be going full time with Primerica. He always told me not to until I had built a good team and was producing a lot, but I wanted to jump right in and give it my all. He said congratulations, and we had a lot of work to do when he got back. Just like that, I was a financial planner.

Chapter 11

YOU'RE GOING TO DIE ANYWAY

When I left Interim, I was a District Leader with Primerica. This means I had recruited at least three people to my team and did $3,000 in premium (sales) in one month. My next promotion would be to Division Leader which was 6 new recruits by $6,000 in premium across my team. In March, I did enough to get promoted to Division. I had a group of young men who were hungry for more. They wanted to be successful and make money, and they knew a lot of people. We went to their parents, and all their parents' friends and their friend's parents and I sold them all life insurance. Since I was the licensed agent, I got paid, and my recruit got credit towards their bonus, which once they got their license they would receive. It was illegal for us to pay an unlicensed agent, so we all start off by giving away some of our market, but if you follow the system correctly, you would soon have your own agents to take out and train and get paid off their markets. I followed this system, and it worked.

There were only a select few of us who were considered full-timers, and we would have a meeting every morning in the office. We ended up calling it the managers meeting because we managed the rest of our teams, with the RVP at the head of the base shop. He was a former Marine and ran the base shop kind of like the military. I responded well to this, and we became friends. We got along great, because we had something in common, and I was a reliable producer for his base shop. I was also coachable and would listen to what he told me to do. He wore a ring the company had given him for making over $100,000 a year. I knew that to have what he has, I needed to do what he did. I became a lot like him, in the way of how I did business. Or at least how he was when he was out in the field producing. Now it was kind of rare for him to go on any appointments, and I don't blame him. He had us, and he made an override off every piece of business we wrote.

Following the system that Primerica had put in place, I won MVP for District Leaders. At our next conference in New Jersey, I would speak in front of 500 people and tell them what I did to get my numbers so high. I would get a lot of awards that trip as well. The key to my success was being prepared for an opportunity. I believe that any degree of success requires a bit of luck. It requires being in the right place at the right time and being knowledgeable and prepared enough to take advantage of that opportunity. I had spent hours each day learning and reading things on my own. I practiced my presentation over and over and over until it was perfect, and I was confident I could do it in front of everyone. I became very fluent in it and was looked at to train the others in the base shop on it. I then met a kid named Nate.

How I met Nate was out of pure luck. I recruited a woman who contracted her daughter, who went to school with Nate, whose major was finance, so she brought him to me. The woman and her daughter were not yet licensed so they could not take Nate out on training appointments, so I did. Nate had a lot of credibility in his market, and he had a great market. Nate was a 6-foot tall black kid who grew up in a good neighborhood and honestly acted whiter than I did. He was a smart kid, but he was young and made frequent mistakes that young people make like I did when I was his age. His father had passed away and did not leave them with much, because he was not covered correctly by life insurance. It caused him and his mother to struggle. This made life insurance an important topic for him, and something he was passionate about. Protecting people from the same disaster that he suffered.

Nate was also an outstanding recruiter. Or rather he had a lot of influence over his friends. He brought them to me, and I recruited them all, so he had a huge team. He made division very quick, which caused me to make regional leader very quick. By May, I was a regional leader running a 10x10 base shop. This means we would recruit 10 new people and do $10,000 in premium on my team per month. I was paid very well for this. I was prepared for the opportunity that Nate brought me and it caused us both to snowball. Nate could have been a really great financial planner, but he was not as coachable. He ended up falling off pretty hard, but his life was hard. His mother was very strict with him, which I understand because he was all she had left. He would need to help her out a lot. She was a very religious woman, who at first did not like me all that much. She thought I was getting Nate into a dangerous lifestyle, until he came home from NJ with a few awards, and he was proud of what he had done. She was then very proud of him and called me to tell me how much she appreciated everything I was teaching her son.

I want to go back to April for a moment and talk about NJ. I wanted Amanda to go with me to listen to my speech, but she had school and was unable to come. I wrote my address and gave it to my RVP to look over. He gave me some advice on what to say, and we drove together to NJ. It was a 6-hour drive, so we had a lot of time to talk about business. I always learned a lot on those trips. From the car ride to the seminar to just talking to the people at the bar, I came back motivated and ready to work hard.

Bill Whittle was the OSJ for us. He was the greatest in the business within Primerica. Everyone knew him, and he was incredibly inspirational. He makes 6 figures a month and doesn't have to work. It is all passive income off the business he built. He donates a ton of money to build churches in other countries. Everyone in the company idolizes him, and I was going to be speaking in front of him. It is the conference he holds every quarter, and he picks 5 people to talk as his MVPs. He also has some guest speakers who are very successful in the business and have built big base shops to tell us how they do it.

Usually I am an excellent public speaker. I got up there in front of Bill and all the other successful people and realized that there was a lot of money looking at me and waiting for me to say something. Bill had his pen to his notebook ready to take notes. The man is one of the most successful people in the company, and probably the country, and he was about to take notes on what I was going to say. He took notes no matter who spoke, because he was respectful of all his guests and always wanted to continue learning. I think listening to him speak is what I miss most about Primerica. I began my speech. I can't even remember what I said but I said something that got loud applause, and though I had more to say, I decided to end it on a good note. I stopped my speech. I felt like I blew it. Little did I know at the time, but I would have another chance.

My numbers were good enough to win MVP at the Division Level as well, even though I wasn't a division for very long, thanks to Nate and his Market. The next trip up to NJ I would be sitting in the front row again and getting awards and speaking. This time I wanted to do better. I played more to the crowd and tried to make it funny. This time Amanda did come and sat next to me up front. She looked beautiful, and everyone thought so. Bill even commented on her beauty and asked what she was doing with me. I think she gave me the confidence to be a better speaker this time. This time I would get a standing ovation and a hug from Bill. Everyone told me that my speech was the best one that day. I was very proud of it and what I had done, and I got to look like a winner in front of the woman of my dreams, which is all I really cared about.

We got back to Rochester and knew that the following week was going to be a big one. We always had a surge of business the week after a trip. Everyone was motivated by the speeches and awards and would talk it up to their friends and family, so we naturally set more appointments. That's all I needed to make a sale. Get people in front of me, and I will close them. I was a closer. Primerica made it easy because we had so many great products for a lower price than most other companies. The reason we could do this is that the company is so big and operates through volume. I learned to compare it to cars. Who makes more money, Honda or Lamborghini? Honda does, but why? Honda sells cheaper cars, but there are many more civics driving around than Lamborghinis. That is how Primerica is able to keep its prices so low. We have many more agents selling many more products, and the company can keep the cost low. We sold term life insurance and taught our clients to invest the difference they would have paid in whole life, so they make out with more money in the long run that they could use for their retirement. Financial freedom is what we sold, and it sold well.

I got promoted again. That month I ran a 15x15 base shop. I had 15 new recruits and did $15,000 in premium. I was now a Sr Regional leader and would get 85% commission off annual premium for everything I sold. The average sale was $1,000 in annual premium, so I would make $850 per sale off my own pen, and an override on my base shop off anything they sold. I had some outstanding agents starting to develop under me, and the override checks were nice. They were like a bonus. Except for the company also gave bonuses, which I usually got as well. The next trip they were giving away was to the Atlantis resort in the Bahamas. I wanted to win it, and I was on track. I just needed to keep my pace. Which I did, and I ended up being the only one in the base shop to win besides the Regional Vice Presidents.

Things were going great, right? So why leave? Why all the problems and how did I end up here? It can be attributed once again to my blind ambition and manic behavior. The office we used at the time we shared with another base shop. It was a small basement office and had no windows. It was not very impressive when you brought any appointments in, and we wanted to change that. Most of our meetings were held at a client's kitchen table. We wanted an office that we could be proud to bring clients to, so we began to look. We found one at the Airport Towers Park. It was a huge office on the 3rd floor with a great view and large windows. It was perfect. It had two separate offices and a large one in between for a conference room. It had a large open room where we could hold meetings and do presentations and eventually, hold licensing class. This was an office we could really grow in. So how did I fit in? The RVP wanted me to be partners with him. He anticipated me getting promoted to Regional Vice President very soon and wanted me to cover half of the office expenses and grow it together.

Without thinking it through, I said yes. All I heard was Regional Vice President and thought about a 6-figure income. Again, I lacked impulse control. Notice a trend? I was so sure I would work hard to make it happen. We moved forward. Unfortunately, I did not have enough at the time to cover half of the initial expenses, and I needed to take out a loan. I took out 10,000. We began shopping for furniture as the place was getting painted. We paid the down payment which was $2400, and I would be responsible for $1200 of rent each month. That was writing one app off my pen, and overriding one app, so I knew I could swing it.

During this time, I also rented a house with my buddy Kevin who moved to NY from Arizona. We served together, and he wanted to move back to NY but had no place to go and didn't have a job. I paid for him to join our company and set him up with licensing class. He was also going to be the office manager for the base shop and earn an hourly wage. We got a house together which we were both responsible for $600 a month. I needed to make over $4000 a month to cover all my bills, including my car and all my insurances. I had done this in the past, but in a new location, it would not be so easy. We held a grand opening party that over 100 people attended, and we got some good business off it initially. The first couple months went well. At this point, I had thought I found my place, and this was what I was meant to do. I thought I would be very successful here and eventually build up that passive income and not have to work so much. I was working 12 hours a day at least, but I did not mind it. We had fun in the office, and out on appointments. We designed training together and ran the Managers meeting.

There was a downside to this business, however, and I would soon find out what it was. Chargebacks. A chargeback is when someone cancels their police before they have had it for a year.

The company already paid you on the policy for the year, so now they need to get their money back from you, and they hit you with a chargeback. What it does is makes it so you can't get paid again until you replace that policy. I would need to write the amount of premium lost until the company would paid me again. This wasn't too bad if you took one every once in a while. One month I took 5 or 6 of them. When an agent quits Primerica, they usually take their market with them, and then the people no longer want the product, and they end up canceling. I had an awful month and had something like $6,000 in chargebacks. Since I had spent all my money on the new office and house, I did not have anything left in my savings. This caused me to not be able to pay my bills. Thank God for Amanda, who bailed me out a couple of times. I could not pay the rent at the office though. My RVP knew what was going on and he was reasonable. He did not bother me for it and just told me to get him what I can, and we would be square.

This was a hole that I could not climb out of though. I was grateful for all the help I was getting, but I needed a way to get myself back on track. I was stressed out and overworked. I was trying to make up the chargebacks, and I would hold really late appointments and go anywhere at any time to try to sell anything to anyone. I became desperate, which usually means lousy business gets done. This would end up hurting me in the long run. Luckily it was almost time to go to the Bahamas on the trip I won. Everything was paid for so I wouldn't have to worry about it, which was good because I had no money. I wanted Amanda to go with me, and Primerica would have paid for her to go too, but she did not get her passport done in time and did not want to be that far away from her son, which I can respect. She dropped me off at the Airport the morning I was leaving, and I said goodbye.

I slept most of the flight there. I changed planes in Miami and would fly directly to Nassau from there. I landed in the Bahamas and waited for my luggage after I cleared customs. I waited for a long time, and something wasn't right. I couldn't get a hold of my RVP because our phones didn't work there, and I didn't have internet access yet. I went up to the counter to ask about my luggage, and they said they made a mistake and it was still in Miami. I was upset, but not surprised. This wasn't the first time an airline lost my luggage, and I'm sure it won't be the last. They said it would get in around 11pm. I had an event I was supposed to be at around 7pm, and now had no clothes to wear. I was in a t-shirt and comfortable athletic pants for my trip. What was I supposed to do now?

I walked outside and looked for transportation to the hotel. I found a guy holding a Primerica sign and got on the bus. It was a 15-minute drive to the hotel from the Airport. Outside the resort, Nassau is a mess. It is run down and looks like the slums. We were also told it was dangerous and not to venture outside the resort. The resort itself was absolutely beautiful. Aqua blue water that you could see right to the bottom of. The hotel itself looked like a giant castle. Inside was a large casino, and many shops. They had their own amusement park, and a few large pools to swim in. It was so big, it took over an hour to walk from one end of the resort to the other. The sun was shining, and it was 80 degrees outside. It was beautiful, and I felt relaxed instantly. That feeling really only lasted a minute.

As I walked into the hotel, I saw my RVP waiting for me. He went up to the desk with me to check in. They asked to put a $500 hold on my card for incidentals. I did not have it, so my RVP was kind enough to put the money on his card. I have no idea what I would have done if he wasn't there.

"Where is your luggage dude?" he asked

"Miami".

"You're kidding."

"Nope, now I have nothing to wear tonight."

"Come to my room after we get you checked in, I have something you can wear."

We walked to the Primerica check-in table, and I picked up my packet for the trip. It had our table numbers for the banquet and awards and an itinerary for where we had to be at certain times. We had one event a day that lasted a couple hours, and the rest of the time was ours to do whatever we wanted.

I noticed that I had a front table at one of the banquets, which means I am getting an award. The trip was enough of an honor for me, but then to be recognized on the trip, is something on a higher level. I was excited about that. The first night was just a welcome party out by the pool. They had a few buffets out so we could eat, and they had a DJ and a dance floor, and everyone mingled and shared stories. I was introduced to a lot of people who were higher up in the company. I felt like somebody there. Some people had said they heard about me and to keep up the good work. Some said I was going to be the next big thing if I just kept working hard. All that praise felt good. Bill even came up to talk to us. We would see him in the gym there every day too. He was big into fitness which I admired. The man was in his late 60s, but he was in better shape than most people in their 20s

We did not stay there very long, and I was tired from the trip, and just wanted to go to bed. I went back to my room and called the Airline to check the status of my luggage. They said it still had not arrived. I was really stressed out and just wanted my stuff, so I had something to wear the next day. Around 11pm there was a knock on my door. It was my luggage. I felt relieved. I spent most of that night talking to Amanda over Facebook messenger. Rochester was getting pounded by a snowstorm, and I was in the sunny Bahamas. I had to rub it in, so I took pictures and posted them. It was mainly for business. People would ask why I was there and I would tell them it was for work, and they would ask what I did, and I would set an appointment for them. The key to success was a lot of recruits. Multiple streams of revenue. Finding what works and duplicating it to the next person. Yes, it was a network marketing platform, but isn't everything if you think about it? This by far was the best one I have found. For $99 you could get your life insurance license and start making money. Low cost buy-in and you had unlimited earning potential if you were willing to work for it. Even though I don't work for them anymore, I still love that company.

The next day we went to our training breakfast. I took a lot of notes because my goal was to make RVP within the next couple of months. After the training, I hit the pool and spent the day outside. Later that night was the awards banquet. I sat at one of the front tables with some of the big names in the company. I had my notebook and pen ready to take any notes that I thought important from the people that sat around me. So much knowledge in one room, I knew I was going to learn something. My name got called for something called "The Future." Only a select few from the company get a future jersey. It signifies being on the right path to being very successful in the company. I was doing all the right things when I needed to do them and felt like I really could make this into something great. The top earners in the company congratulated me and took pictures with me. It felt terrific. It felt like I belonged. Everyone in Primerica is so supportive of each other. It is unlike any other financial company out there, and I recommend it to anyone who has a personal drive to succeed. Just pace yourself, and don't outgrow your reach like I did. I often take on more than I can handle in hopes that I will develop myself and grow or adapt to the challenge.

This is good in small doses, but realistically some of the things that I do are impossible without having money saved up.

Can you think of the irony here? I was a successful financial planner in the eyes of the company, but was also broke. All my money went to the large number of bills I had, and I never had any left over for anything else. This was no way to live, and it began to eat away at me. I fell behind in my bills, especially my car. When I returned home from the Bahamas, Amanda picked me up at the Airport and drove me home. When we got to my driveway, my car was nowhere in sight.

"Kevin, where is my car?"

"I don't know man. It was here this morning when I left for work. Did you pay the bill?"

"Yeah. I am pretty sure I did."

I had thought I paid my last car bill, so I called the police. They looked into it and called me back. They said the car had been repossessed by the bank. The repo company is smart. They did this on a Friday so I would have to wait over the weekend to get it out since they weren't open on the weekend, and they could collect a couple extra days of fees. I called the bank the next day and was transferred around to many different departments to tell me my last payment didn't go through and I needed to pay $1800 to get my car back. I did not have that much, so Amanda, who had recently received her taxes back helped me out. I felt bad, because she wanted to save that money to buy a house with me. I didn't want her to help me, but she insisted and said I would do the same for her, which is true, but only because I feel that's how it should be.

The next day I would need to be picked up and taken to work, so I told my RVP, and he came and got me. We worked on training that day to convey to the team all that was talked about on the trip and what we could do to get more people to go on the next one. I made a PowerPoint based on all the notes I took. We went over it all with the base shop, and they asked questions. As I looked out into the large opened room, I realized that our team was shrinking. We had fewer people in training than we usually do, which is a sign that people have given up and this is no longer important to them. Most of them were my people. Right now, I needed all the people I could get to help me get out of this hole I was in, but one by one they all dropped off. More stress ensued.

I was just about at my breaking point. I hadn't been paid in over a month, all my bills were past due, and my RVP was riding me for production. My well had dried up. I had just received an award saying I was the future of the company and now I can't even write one app. What was I going to do? I laid in bed at night and would stare off into space. I wondered when the last time I was honestly happy was. What was the point of all this? Can I continue on this path or did I need to find something else? I found some hard truths. The last time I was happy was when I was training people. The fitness industry before I turned it into a business. Just writing programs and helping people achieve their goals. I wanted to get back to that. Back to something simpler. I believe I looked for a way out of Primerica and a way out of the hard situation I was in.

To make matters worse, Kevin was about to move back to Arizona. His ex-fiancé came to visit him, and he realized he still loved her and wanted to be with her. He asked me if I would let him out of the lease so he could move back to Arizona. I told him yes. I knew I wouldn't be ok paying all of it by myself, but he was a friend of mine, and I wanted him to be happy. The financial thing put a strain on our relationship as well, and it was probably best for our friendship if he moved anyway. I was not sure how I was going to do all this, so I began to apply for jobs in the fitness industry. A girl I knew that I almost hired at my old gym sent me a Facebook message. She told me that she saw my resume, and she is the manager at Orange Theory Fitness. She asked if I wanted to interview. I said yes. Before that, I had never heard of Orange Theory Fitness, but I wanted to go check it out.

My RVP then broke my trust. Honestly, it wasn't even that bad because he didn't really do anything to me, he just inadvertently put me in a bad personal situation that involved an agent of mine. I won't go into details to protect those involved, but it was the out I was looking for. I think I just used it as an excuse to get out of the business. It did not really affect me financially or personally, but I needed a change because I was drowning, and I used that to facilitate change. I went into my office one last time to clean out my desk. My RVP was there with another agent of mine, who worked for the building. He was changing the locks. As if I was going to break in and vandalize the place. He sat on the couch in my office as I cleaned out my desk.

"So That's it?" He asked

"Yes. I am done."

"What happened? I thought we were friends."

"We were. I am just done, man. I can't do it anymore. I can't deal with the drama. I can't keep going further into debt. I just can't do it."

"Can I stop recording this? Like you aren't going to attack me or anything right?" he asked pulling his phone out.

"Yeah, don't be ridiculous. I don't want to hurt you."

"So, it is mainly financial trouble. That's the reason you are leaving?"

"It's a lot of things. That is probably the biggest one though."

"Ok. I can respect that. You have to do what you have to do. You are really good at this so maybe we can work something out."

"I don't know, I think I am just done."

"What if we drop you down to a Division leader again, and you just work part-time? That way you can build back up and not have all the responsibility on you."

"I will think about it."

I finished cleaning out my desk and went home. My mind was already made up. I could not show my face back in that office again. I knew that I wouldn't be able to. The people would not look at me the same way now, and if they knew what I was going through they would lose faith in the company. The best thing for everyone was if I just disappeared. More lost friendships and relationships. I felt doomed to be alone, or circulate the people in my life every couple of years or so. I began to feel like I would not find a place to belong.

Although it ended with hardship, I do not regret my time in Primerica. It taught me so many things about business and finances that I can use to better my future. I now know how things should be done, and how to make the most out of every dollar. These are skills I would use at the beginning of my next business venture, but then lose once I needed to figure out a way to expand. With each business venture, I learn more and more. Each time I fail is a lesson that has taught me what not to do next time. Primerica gave me a lot of good times with great people, and if I had to do it all over again knowing how it would end, I think I would make the same choices. I learned a lot from some very successful people, and those experiences are invaluable to me. Bill Whittle taught me the key to success is to always continue to learn. The man was already successful but still took more notes at his own training than anyone else in the room. Humble yourself, because it doesn't matter how good you are, you can always learn something and be better.

I planned to work and go to school at RIT. I would use my GI bill and get paid to get an education and work an easy part-time job on the side. Sounded like a good plan, and if I followed through with it, it probably would have been, but an opportunity arose, and my ambition would get the best of me one more time.

Chapter 12

INSERT A QUARTER TO KEEP PLAYING

At this point, my life felt like a video game. One where I kept dying and had to start over. As if I was in an arcade and had to keep spending money to stay alive and continue the journey. To recap, I had joined the Air Force, got married, had a daughter, got divorced, left the military, started a business, it went under, started another business, it went under, worked for a healthcare company and quit to run my own financial business, which also went under. I had my car repossessed and was about to lose my house and move back in with my mom. I have started over so many times, and it was getting frustrating. Little did I know, I was going to have to do it all over again too.

I was sick the day of my interview at Orange Theory but did not want to pass up the opportunity, so I went to my interview anyway. I walked into the studio and immediately realized this was not like any gym I had ever seen before. Ashley stood at the desk and welcomed me to the studio. She took me on a short tour. The studio was small, and the workouts were class based. There was a little open section with weights, TRX bands, and weights on one side of the room, and treadmills and water rowers on the other side. The concept of Orange theory fitness is not a new one, but they put their own spin on it. Essentially it is High-Intensity Interval Training (HIIT) where you increase your heart rate into the "Orange" zone for 12 to 24 minutes per class and then recover to the "green zone" or active recovery for at least 25 minutes per class. It is a system that is designed to lose weight and works well at doing that.

I interviewed for the Sales associate position. I would be selling new memberships and taking care of the current members. During our interview, Ashley asked me if ever wanted to be a trainer again. I said someday, but I wasn't ready to get back into it yet. I got the job and was going to start on Monday. I would work the day shift, from 7:30am to 3:30pm. It was an easy job where I would make phone calls to interested parties and set up their first complimentary class. There was a format for us to follow when trying to sell someone and it was one I was familiar with. Mostly it was the same as Professional selling skills. We asked questions about their goals and what they were doing now, and then told them how we could help them achieve those goals.

I could sell the Air Force, and I could sell life insurance. I have sold fitness before so this job would not be incredibly challenging for me. Or at least it shouldn't be. Again, I planned to work until school started and then drop down to part-time. That is what I wanted to do, and it was a good path to be on. So where did it all go wrong? At the time I thought it was all going right. It was going so right that I didn't need school anymore.

I started working for OTF in March 2016. My first day I woke up early, got ready, and left the house. I walked through the doors about 20 minutes before the start of my shift. A man stood at the desk as I walked in.

"Are you here to take a class?" He asked as I walked through the door.

"No. It's my first day. I am here to work."

"I'm so sorry. Matt, right?"

"Yes. I know I am a bit early."

"That's ok. Go ahead and clock in, and we will get started anyway."

"Ok. How do I do that." I asked.

"Right…let me show you."

He was from corporate, and he would be the one to start training the new girl and me. She was a member of Orange theory first and then decided to work part-time, which meant she could work out there for free. She had a respectable full-time job and was a very motivated individual who was set on accomplishing her goals.

The computer system OTF used was Mindbody. The same system I had used before, and I was familiar with how it worked. I set the whole thing up for my gym. I told our trainer that, and he let me skip some of the training. The first hour was going over online training videos to learn how to do our daily tasks. Then he would show us how to make phone calls and how to handle an Intro (Someone coming to class for the first time). What made OTF different was their use of heart rate monitors. You could see your heart rate up on the screen the whole time and watch how you were doing to make sure you were hitting the correct zones at the right time to maximize your results.

The price of membership was costly depending on what level you wanted. They also had a 30-day cancellation policy, and you needed to buy a heart rate monitor when you signed up. If I were running that business, I would give away the first heart rate monitor because you know they will be a member for at least two months and that will more than pay for the cost of the monitor. It shows better customer service and would probably keep members there longer. Also, if the thing didn't work right, at least it was free so they couldn't complain too much about it. Instead, they sold these for $100. People were willing to pay it though. OTF does know what it's doing because they have expanded internationally in just 5 short years, so people are willing to pay, and they have a pretty solid business model.

Being back in the fitness industry would mean I would hear people put themselves down for how they look, or what they could not do. I believe it is a defense mechanism. I have had people I trained tell me they messed up, and they need to do better but go right back to the things they were doing. As if taking responsibility for their failure is a way to deflect the blame or consequences. People would come to me and say, "I know I messed up." Or "I know I need to do better" to deflect anything I might say to them. Perhaps they fear the consequences or what I would say to them, so they confess their shortcomings before I have the opportunity to talk about it. I have learned to take this one step further. If someone came up to me with one of those excuses, basically saying they weren't strong enough to do what needs to be done, I would then look at them and ask, "what are we going to do about it?" If they wanted to take responsibility for it, then I would make them take responsibility and come up with a solution. Once we agreed on a good solution that we believed could work, I would then ask, "Can I hold you to this?" They would always reply yes. They wanted to achieve these goals, no matter what they were, and they gave me permission to hold them accountable. I would also give them permission to hold me responsible and tell them if I am not holding up my end of the bargain to please let me know.

My end goal was always to empower people. I wanted to show people they were capable of more than they knew. I wanted to give them the tools to succeed and set them in the right direction but watch them grow and learn along the way. The best compliment I could ever get is when someone tells me they don't need me anymore. I know that if someone was able to go off on their own and use the tools that they learned to better their life, then I did a good job. That is how I wanted my business to operate. I wanted to have new clients coming in to replace people that cycled out because they now had the drive and the knowledge to do it themselves. This did not always happen, and a perfect plan is altered by the reality of the world. What usually ended up happening was people would develop a dependency, and it would be hard to cycle them out. They thought that they couldn't get results without me. I needed to figure out how to change this. I was unsuccessful.

I will get to my business in a moment, and my transition from working OTF to working full time for myself (again). One problem I had with Orange Theory was the pay. I got paid $10 an hour plus commissions. It would have been nice if the commissions were decent, but they weren't. We would make a sale and on average get between $8 and $15 per sale. On average, I made a little over $500 every two weeks. Coming from the finance world, and even my work at Interim Healthcare, this was a huge pay cut. I knew that this was just a temporary move for me. It was my foot back in the door of the fitness industry. It would allow me to talk to the trainers and learn what was new out there, and what trainers had emerged over the years. It allowed me to study a platform that was not common and learn how they became successful. It was a learning experience for me, which made it worth more than any amount they could have paid me. At least that is what I told myself. Who knows if I actually believed that?

A couple times a week I would work with the new girl in the morning. She got to know me and learned about my past and learned that I was a personal trainer. She was a larger woman who had goals to lose 100 lbs. She had already lost a lot on her own with kickboxing and OTF. She felt that she had hit a wall and was no longer seeing results, and told me that if I wanted to be a personal trainer again, she would be my first client. I did not read too much into it at first. I had not even thought about training people again yet. I was not sure if I was ready. She would talk to me again about it and tell me that she was serious and wanted to train with me. I began to start thinking about what I could do. I would need to find a place to train.

I began my search for a place to train part-time. I googled small personal training studios and started to make calls. I looked at a few places and talked to the owners. The one I picked was not the most beautiful gym I looked at and not even the cheapest, but the owner was the best person out of all of them. That was important to me due to my past. He had a genuine kindness about him. He is a shorter man, but extremely muscular. Don't let his small stature give you ideas about this man's strength. He is stronger than most men twice his size. He is a very dedicated fitness professional, and also a teacher for a local high school. He impressed me on all fronts, and I knew I wanted to work in his gym.

The rent was $300 a month, so I was going to need to figure out what I was going to charge to make it worth my time to train people. He gave me the rest of the month for free and told me to start paying him on the first. This allowed me to build up my clientele, so I was not losing money. I had to come up with a name for my business so I could market it. A lot of personal trainers will just use their own name and market themselves, but I knew to stand out and succeed you needed to be different. I wanted to keep the military theme to my business since that is where my passion for training people all started. I ended up on the name Gruntz Fitness. I submitted the paperwork for an LLC and bought the domain name gruntzfitness.com. Then I went back through my original business plan and made a bunch of changes to reflect my current situation. I believe a good business plan will always be changing to adapt to current circumstances, but the core of the business plan should remain the same. The values and end goals should never change, but the direction we take to get there could.

I designed the website myself. It wasn't a flashy or very good website. It didn't have many pages and was designed to just get information out and set up a consultation. I then took to social media to try to get some more clients. It wouldn't take long for me to fill up all the available time I had. The girl I worked with was a big part of that. Her success with me was what propelled my business forward at first. She got results because I became obsessed about being the best again. It had been a while since I had trained anyone, and I needed to make sure I still knew what I was doing. I went back to the basics. (The old familiar pattern had started back up again)

I reread my old NASM book and did a lot of research on their phase system, and the different types of exercise I could do with her. I also had to keep in mind that in the beginning, she wouldn't be able to do everything because of where she was physically, so I had to make modifications and adjustments. I spent hours researching, and then going back over my nutrition book as well to make sure I developed the best plan I could for her. I needed to make one that worked for her. She was my first client since I got back into it, and she was paying me, so I needed to be worth the money. Results and excellent customer service was the only way I was going to grow my business. An LLC, a Website, and some Facebook advertisements don't mean you know what you are doing, so I needed to make sure I could deliver on my promises.

I searched for the best software to keep track of my clients and also relay to them a good plan of action. I found TotalCoaching. This app allowed me to input a meal plan for clients, and load all of their workouts. It would track their calorie intake and expenditure so I could use my knowledge and math to calculate how much weight they should be losing each week and make minor adjustments as needed. I spent hours getting to know the software and making her plan. Once it was done, she could look at it all on an app on her phone or go on the website and see it. There are so many trainers in Rochester, and I knew I needed to go above and beyond to separate myself from them. I have seen a lot of bad trainers who regularly cancel on their clients, or don't really know what they are doing and push their clients into an injury or give bad advice. I never wanted to be one of those trainers.

Results came quick. I believe her first full week with me she lost about 10 lbs. She was happy and was telling everyone. Two of her friends both contacted me shortly after. They wanted to get ready for a bodybuilding show and needed help. They had started training with someone else, but that person canceled on them half of their appointments, and they no longer wanted to work with them. I held consultations for them, and they signed up with me. One of them ended up sending her boss to me, who only wanted a meal plan at first. Then decided to train once a week. Eventually, that turned into three times a week, and she loved the results she got. She introduced me to the owner of another club in Rochester.

The woman who owned the club was extremely friendly and ran a lot of programs out of her studio, which was set up for different types of classes. The studio was large, and very clean, and had a fantastic Juice bar in the front. She wanted to start up a program that she had done before to get people to jump-start their fitness goals in the summer. It was an 8-week program, and I would run the nutrition side of it. Initially, this paid pretty well but would be a lot of work. We ended up with a group of 25 people, and I needed to make meal plans for all of them. The way I did my meal plans were based on people's macronutrients, which is the amount of protein, carbs, and fat someone should have based on their body type. I did this for everyone. The people that listened to the guidance of myself and the others involved in the program saw great success. There were also people on the other end of that spectrum who didn't want to listen to anything we said and didn't understand why they didn't see any results.

There are so many people out there who want to see results but aren't interested in putting in the work. Some people believe that if they hire a personal trainer, the results will just happen through magic or something. I am very upfront with everyone and tell them that the meal plan will not be fun. You will be eating to fuel your body and get results. You will feel better, but don't expect there to be pizza and beer on the plan. People would try to alter the program all the time or ask me if they could have something different. As a race, humans have gotten away from eating for survival and now eat for pleasure. They want what tastes good and will over-eat and then wonder why they put on so much weight or can't lose weight. Your weight problems can be boiled down to one simple thing. Math. Yes, math. If you are putting in more calories than you are expending in a given day, then your body will store those calories as fat, or muscle depending on the nutrient and your level of activity. If you are burning more calories than you are taking in, then your body will use your stored fat as energy, because the energy must come from somewhere. If you want to get really basic about it, then we can break it right down to the most basic numbers, and that is calories. Now, there are different equations to use if you want to maximize your results and that is where calculating out your MACROS for your goals comes into play. If you don't know how to do that, then seek out a professional and do your homework.

As the program became more popular and my personal clientele began to grow, I ended up running out of time slots. I would now train clients before I went to work at Orange Theory and after I got out. I was making more money training part-time than I was full time at OTF, but OTF had stability, so I stayed. That and I liked all the people there. They had a lot of great members, and the job wasn't too hard. I still had my goal of going to school in the fall as well. Then the problems started.

I had always tried to keep my personal training business and OTF separate. I never talked about training people when I was at work at OTF because I didn't want it to be seen as a conflict of interest. I still sold OTF memberships and did my job. The problem was people were learning about me from my clients, and from seeing posts on Facebook, so they would come up to me at OTF and ask me about it. They would ask me what I did and how much I charged, and where I trained out of and I always kept my answers short and never added any information or tried to set up an appointment. I could tell that this line of questioning from the members was starting to bother Ashley, and she didn't want to lose members to me. That was never my intent.

My first client and coworker became a bit upset with working at Orange Theory. They kept changing things, and she no longer needed to work out there because she was working with me, so I think that had a lot to do with her decision to put her 2 weeks in. I will never forget that day because she told me I should put mine in too because my business is growing, and I didn't need Orange Theory. I still did not plan to put it in on that day and wanted the stability for a little while longer. When Ashley came into work that day, she asked me how my client was. I said she seemed okay. She told me she put her two weeks in. Obviously, I already knew this. She then looked at me and asked if I wanted to put my two weeks in too. She said she was building a team and needed people who were going to stick around, and she knew that my business was growing and didn't think I would be there much longer. It felt like I was being asked to leave. As a business owner and manager, I don't blame her for putting that on me. I would have done the same thing. Keeping me employed there could have had an adverse effect on business, and she was doing her job and removing the problem professionally. I agreed and put my two weeks in that day. Now I was going to be full time as a trainer (Again). I would have more slots opened and would need to make sure I could fill them if I were going to make enough money to pay all my bills and be self-sufficient again.

I learned from Orange Theory how the fitness industry was changing from when I was a trainer. I learned what the new fads were and how to stay relevant. I also learned how a relatively new workout facility became so popular so quickly. I took some ideas for my business and learned some things that I would never want to do. I recommend Orange Theory fitness for anyone looking to lose weight in a group setting, with a lot of support from your peers and trainers.

Chapter 13

THIS TIME WILL BE DIFFERENT

I was once told that the definition of insanity was doing the same thing over and over and expecting different results. Hello, I am insane. By now I should have noticed the pattern I was in. Ambition, to business, to small quick amounts of success, to making new and great friends, to self-sabotage, to losing all my money, my business, and my friends. This would be the fourth or arguably the fifth time that I would enter into this pattern. A clinical psychologist could describe my behavior of periods of mania followed by periods of depression, which is a textbook definition of bipolar 1 disorder. Although I have never been officially diagnosed with this.

Here I was. Back at it again. Only this time I was doing it alone. I preferred it that way. I could run things the way I wanted to without debate. When I first started Gruntz Fitness I had no idea it would take off the way that it did. I still planned on only training a few people a day and making some extra cash. How could I have known that people would respond so positively to it?

My day now had some free time between the hours of 7am and 3pm. I was going to be able to fill these slots with new clients. There was no shortage of clients to fill those spots. Before I knew it, I was at a total of 30 clients for myself. This was between training and nutritional guidance. I was making between $6,000 and $8,000 a month, but I worked nonstop. It was starting to get to me, and I knew if I were going to continue to grow I would need help. Amanda and I had a mutual friend, and I took my daughter to his son's birthday party. It was there he told me that his wife was in the process of getting certified as a trainer and I should hire her to help me out. I thought that since we were friends, and she always seemed like a hard worker that it sounded like a good idea. She was not certified yet though, so at first, I would have her shadow me.

She would shadow me once a week for a month until she took her certification. I usually had her shadow me at night because she worked during the day. She was a manager, so she had management experience which was vital to me if my business was going to grow. My first client was not ok with her shadowing me during our sessions and told me she thought I was trying to pawn her off. I told her that was not the case, but for some reason, she did not believe me. It ended up causing her to leave, and she went off on her own for about a month before coming back to train.

I started to let my success get to me. I had people jumping ship from other gyms and trainers to come train with me. I was making a lot of money, and my presence in the Rochester area was growing. People were starting to know who we were. I wanted to be an influence to others that had ambition and drive like me, so I wrote and published an article of my ten business practices that I utilized to become successful. Even though my business failed, I still believe that these are useful practices, and they did not cause me to fail. What caused me to fail was the fact that I grew too fast and made some impulsive decisions about what my next steps should be. I made the wrong decisions that ended up being very costly. It was kind of presumptuous of me to assume that others would want my advice. The article read as follows:

It is amazing what 1 year can do. At the beginning of 2016, I worked for a financial marketing company. I was not happy with what I was doing, and there didn't seem to be a way out. I was very depressed and had no direction. I thought to myself one day "when was the last time you were truly happy with what you did" The answer was when I was a personal trainer. (This blog post could be a lot longer if I went into the old days when I was a trainer and had a gym, but that might be a story for another time.) I knew I needed to get back into the fitness Industry. I applied to work at some local gyms and landed an Interview with Orange Theory Fitness. My role there was not to train people but being a different type of fitness studio, I saw an opportunity to learn. I began working there in March. I had no intentions at the time to get back into training people anytime soon. A co-worker of mine had some large fitness goals and was talking to me about them. She had convinced me to train her. (Its funny how one small decision can transform your whole life) Feeling a bit rusty, I dusted off my old books, I began to do research after work and wanted to develop the best program I could for her. She was trusting me with her fitness goals. At the end of April, I began to train her part-time after I got out of work at Orange Theory Fitness. She began to tell others about me. By the end of May, I was juggling 20 clients and my job at Orange Theory Fitness. I began to realize that what I had was no longer a hobby, but a business. I spent the rest of this year developing my business and growing an amazing team of employees. We are now in the process of opening up Gruntz Fitness LLC Flagship location. A 9100 Sq Ft location in Henrietta NY. The first of what we believe will be many locations to come. So how did we do it? Below is the 10 Business practices that I have used this year to transform myself from a depressed financial planner to one of the fastest growing fitness businesses in our area today!

1. Turn your passion into your paycheck- You have to love what you do and dedicate your time to becoming really good at it! Don't start a business to make money. Start it to be happy with what you are doing every day! (The money will come...but not at first) This will require you to get very comfortable with the uncomfortable. Maybe working two jobs and losing sleep.

2. Be consistent- Every morning I wake up at 4am, get ready, and go train my first client. I know when I leave in the morning I won't be back until 8pm. Every day I do the same tasks that have made me successful in the first place. You can't waiver and expect to get the same results.

3. Goal setting- Doing the same core things every day is important, but you also need to add something productive to your day. Did you do something today that will bring you closer to what you want tomorrow? What plans have you made for the future? Consistency is key, but complacency kills.

4. Sacrifice- Don't give up what you want for what you want now. There are a lot of things I want now or things I want to do that I am putting off because it would set the business back. Some days this is very hard, and if

there are days you don't feel like giving up, then you aren't doing it right. In the end, it will all be worth it. I am fortunate (sort of) that I am a disabled vet and receive a check from the VA each month. It isn't a lot of money, but it is enough to pay my personal bills and have a little left over. This has allowed me to not draw a paycheck from my business so all the money we make can be reinvested into the growth of the business. Be prepared to be poor for a little while until your business gets to where it needs to be.

5. Surround yourself with the right people- No one, and I mean no one, has ever obtained success alone. It takes a team of goal-oriented, like-minded individuals with a great work ethic to propel you forward. This could be the hardest part. Not everyone you bring on will be that person, but when you find the right people make sure you include them in your plans for the future. Take care of them and learn to delegate. There are not enough hours in the day to do everything you need to get done, so once you have people you can trust with your business, give them tasks you would normally do so you can focus your attention on moving forward.

6. MORE PEOPLE- Seriously…people are the key to success. Not only the ones you hire but your target market. First, you need to figure out who that is. You may have a great product or a great idea, but if no one knows about it than it is a wasted idea. Once you figure it out, then get the word out. We do a lot of advertising on social media, and you will rarely find me out on the town without wearing something that says Gruntz Fitness on it. The more people that see your brand and know that you exist, the more traffic you will drive to your business.

The best way to reach more people is through the people you already have. Word of mouth is huge, so once you have clients make sure you treat them very well and do a good job, so they tell their friends. Don't get clients and then move on to the next. You need to spend some of your energy and efforts on retention and keeping people happy!

7. Develop Good Business Relationships (Local) - Running a business means you will have to do business with other businesses. You can't expect to do payroll, signs, taxes, marketing, website design, etc. all yourself. Develop strong relationships with good people. They will care about the success of your business not just because you are a good, kind-hearted person, but also because they will continue to get money from you while you are operating. This can help perpetuate your name and give you a good reputation in your area. So always be kind!

8. Always be kind! Might as well start this one off where the last one ended. Being kind and fair is important. No one will tell someone to go see you if you are mean to them. Even if your feelings, morals, and values don't mesh up with who you are dealing with, you need to separate yourself from your own emotions and realize that everyone is different. We all come from different places and have different views. If someone so different from you is coming to do business with you, then you are doing something right. Don't let emotions get in the way of a good thing (I have done this before, and it doesn't end well)

9. Be Firm- Being Kind and being weak are two different things. Some people will mistake the two. I can be the nicest person in the world until you do me wrong. Don't

let anyone walk all over you and your business. There is a time for compromise, but if there are people who are just trying to take advantage of you, and it will end up hurting you or your business, then you need to let them know and remove yourself from that situation. There are a lot of poisonous people out there. Don't let them near your organization, or they will bring it down. It only takes one person to topple a great company. So be careful and be observant.

10. Have Fun! This is your business, your passion, your life. If you don't have fun while doing it, then you have already started to fail. Not every day will be fun, but overall when you look at what you are doing, you should be happy with it. It shouldn't always feel like work! There should be days where you say to yourself "I can't believe I get paid to do this." If you can keep that attitude and maintain your work ethic, then you can make it through the hard times. (There will be hard times…I didn't write about them but trust me…they happen) When I go to work, there are clients I train that brighten my day, and I have such a great time training them. You can laugh, joke, and have fun and still get a lot of work done. A happy work environment is often the most productive because your staff will want to be there. (And so will your clients!)

This obviously isn't the end all, be all to having a successful business. In fact, what works for me may not work for you at all. Just like in the fitness industry, there are many different ways to achieve your goals. Also, I do way more than 10 things a day to keep my business afloat, and there are other contributing factors that help, such as having the support of my loving girlfriend,

family, friends, and Sunday Football (the only day I take off....
try to get me to work a Sunday. Nope. We all need a day for our
sanity)

I believe that the drive has to be there. The ambition. It has
to be something at the core of you to succeed. If it is not there,
then don't try this. This is not a life meant for everyone. I gave
up a 40-hour work week for an 80-hour work week just so I could
be my own boss. If 80 hours doesn't appeal to you...don't start.
You aren't ready yet. At my core, I love to help people. That is
why I love this industry, and that is why I took the time (ON A
SUNDAY) to write this. If you are just starting out or want to
talk business and need some help, then reach out to me. I will
help anyone who is trying their hardest to make their dreams
come true...because I am trying my hardest to make mine come
true and I know how it feels. I may not have all the answers you
are looking for, and I am still open to taking advice from more
successful people than me because you always need to keep
learning, but if I can help you, then I will.

Good Luck out there, Matt

That was it, and it got a lot of positive feedback. I felt like I
was inspiring people. Maybe I was, maybe I wasn't. I really did
try though. I have always wanted to be "somebody." Where did
my obsession to matter come from? I have wanted to be the
one people go to for help or look up to. A positive role model
in a society that has been so negative. We need a little light in
the world, and I wanted to provide that. The darkness of our
community is enough to suffocate the oxygen from any flame,
and so, for now, my light has burned out. The good thing about
fire is it can always be re-lit. I plan to come back with a vengeance
and be everything I know I can be, but until then I will sit here
in the dark.

Once my intern was ready to start working, we sat down to discuss the specifics. We had to come up with an employee structure that would work for both of us. It was after a night of training, and we were the only two left in the building. We walked back into our small locker room "office" and sat at the table.

"Ok, let's get down to business," I said as I pulled out the plan I had laid out for her. "I am going to give you 100% commission on the first month a new person signs with us, so you make all of that up front, and then 50% after that. I will pay your rent here and pay for the systems we use to track clients and make programs. I will help you obtain new clients in the beginning and hold all initial interviews until you are comfortable doing it yourself."

As I was explaining this, I could see a troubling look on her face.

"What's wrong?" I asked.

"So, I only get paid if I bring in new clients? That is not going to work for me." She said.

"Why not? Are you not planning on bringing in clients?"

"I am, but I need something that is guaranteed, so I can pay my bills."

"How much do you need?" I asked, which was a dangerous question and started a chain reaction that would eventually lead to my downfall.

She gave me a number, and we settled on that. I would pay her a salary. Not hourly. She would make pretty good money part-time, and I would take on all the risk. I believed she was worth it though. Then when she became full time, I would pay her $3,000 a month. For a new trainer in the Rochester area who just became certified and had no prior experience, this was unheard-of. She was a friend though, and I figured if I took care of her she would work hard and take care of me.

My friend started working for me in July. Having an employee brought on a bunch of new challenges for me. I had to run payroll because she didn't want to have to worry about a 1099 and preferred to get a W-2. I would also need to pay payroll tax and software costs. This meant that I took a massive pay cut in hiring her, but I figured it would all pan out when she brought in some new clients. I taught her how I got clients and showed her what I did during a consultation which had a very high success rate. I was training her to be a manager because someday I would need one to manage the other trainers I planned on having.

A month went by, and she was starting to get frustrated because she had no new consultations. The consultations she did set up ended up canceling on her, and she became really hard on herself. I told her to keep doing what she was doing, and it would all fall into place. I was still positive on the revenue side of the house, so I didn't stress about it too much just yet. The following month she got her first client. The weight and pressure were lifted off of her, and she began to design her clients program, with my help. The first one is always the hardest, but after that, if you do a good job, then others will come. They sure did.

Both I and my new trainer were bringing in a lot of business. It got to the point where I told her to go full time because we were so busy. We were both booked all day and bringing in over $10,000 a month. We even had our own clothing line that our clients were sporting and getting us new clients. So now, we both worked all the time, and we knew we needed to find more help. I put my feelers out for good trainers to hire. I ended up hiring a girl that did a modeling shoot for us and was a friend of a friend. She had a huge following on social media and was a competent trainer. Her name was Claire.

Both Claire and my head trainer (my friend) were strong independent type females, so instantly there was a bit of conflict. Claire didn't like that the head trainer was her direct supervisor and would often come to me for things, which I didn't really mind, but in the end, the chain of command needed to be respected. Everyone that Claire trained loved training with her. She was a lot of fun and had a good personality. She was also a competitor and was the posing coach for our competitors. With her social presence, she could have propelled our business so much further than it was already. She just had to use it. She did not use it correctly. Like my head trainer, she was tasked with bringing in new clients. This would prove to be difficult for her as well. She would work with the head trainer and try to get people in the door but ultimately fell short. I did not mind all that much though because we did have a lot of clients and were still on the positive side of revenue.

With two employees and focus on expanding my reach in the fitness industry, I decided to hire an assistant, to help me with paperwork and marketing so I could focus more on the clients, which is what I really loved to do. A client introduced me to her friend who had been an assistant for a couple of businesses before. These businesses are no longer in business, which I should have seen as a red flag, but she had an impressive resume, so I gave her the job. If I had to pinpoint a moment when everything started to slip away from me, this I believe would be that moment. She seemed like she meant well, but she was very manipulative, and two-faced, and would do and say anything to get people to like her. The more I got to know her the less I liked her as a person. She was good at marketing and always got everything I needed her to do acomplished, but there was still something about her that I didn't trust.

It got to the point where the 2000 sq. Ft location we were training out of became crowded. I ventured out looking for investors and a new place. I found a 9000 sq. Ft location that was perfect and put money down on it and signed a lease. The lease was a 5-year lease with a personal guarantee. A sane person would look at the decision I made and tell me I was insane for making it. I had verbal agreements with people who wanted to back me with money, and they said they believed in me. I trusted them. I was wrong to do so. In their defense, they would have been wrong to give me the money, so I do not blame them for their eventual decision to back out.

Claire was going through a hard time in her life, and this caused her to be late for some clients. At first, I did not mind all that much. It was a slap on the wrist and don't do it again type of punishment. She made it a habit though, and I sat her down to talk to her about what was going on. I just wanted to be on the same page as her, and let her know that the other trainers and clients counted on her to be to work on time, so the clients could get the training they paid for. She was very understanding and apologetic. For me, I am all about crisis management and making sure my people are ok, and business can go on. She did get better for a little while, but one day she did not show up at all. This left us in an awful spot, and two clients ended up training themselves. I know now that she had been going through something, and had a good reason for not showing up, but I could no longer let it affect my business and had to let her go. My head trainer and assistant had been pushing for me to fire her before because they did not like her. I think it is because she was real. She never put on a fake face, and always spoke her mind, and they did not like that about her. I appreciate people like that over people who are fake and pretend to be my friend any day. Claire will now be the manager of a kickboxing studio and has offered to help me out time and time again after I let her go.

The day I let Claire go she owned up to her mistakes. She did not give me a hard time, and she apologized for the trouble she had caused. She took responsibility, and I respect that a lot. I also appreciate the fact that she has offered to help me so much after she left, whenever I was short a trainer. She even offered to work for free. If I had to do it all over again, I would have kept Clair and fired the rest. She has good character qualities, and a lot of potential and I wish her the best.

Now I was down a trainer and needed to find another one fast. My assistant said she knew a great trainer, and she would talk to her about coming in for an interview. This trainer worked at another gym only making $13 an hour. According to my assistant, she was an outstanding trainer and had a large following of people who would probably come with her to our business if we hired her. I had my head trainer conduct the interview because I wanted her to build a staff that she was comfortable with and could manage well, so it was vital that they meshed well. She was also in charge of scheduling and needed to make sure the applicant's availability would match what we needed them for.

My head trainer told me the interview went well, and she wanted to hire the girl. She said that she needed a couple weeks to work the schedule out with her other job, so we gave her a couple weeks. If I were smart, I would have just stopped there and continued to grow before I hired anyone else, but we had other trainers interested in the position and my head trainer set up interviews with them. One of them was a trainer from Orange Theory named David. David is by far one of the best trainers I have ever met. He has so much passion and knowledge for the industry and is really committed to his clients. I could not pass up the opportunity to have him work for us, so I hired him as well. This is where I should have stopped for real. I now have two new employees, one making $22 an hour and the other making $25, on top of the $3000 salary I was giving my head trainer. The business was bringing in $12,000 to $14,000 a month at this point, but it all went to business expenses, and I did not even pay myself. This caused my own personal finances to fall into peril.

Except I had one other person, who wanted to work for me. She was also not certified yet and was a client of ours. She had a passion for the business and was not making any money as a financial planner, which I know is tough because I did it. I brought her on as a paid intern. If I were smart, I would have done an unpaid internship like I did for my head trainer. This may have motivated her to get her certification faster, which she never ended up getting with me. I paid her $15 an hour, which is more than anyone would ever pay an inexperienced and non-certified trainer. I overpaid my employees. I knew I was doing it, and I did it because I valued them and liked them as people. I hurt myself and the business to make sure they were taken care of because I figured if I took care of them then they would work harder for me.

This mindset came from my military background. I always wanted to make sure my troops were taken care of. If I did a good job as a leader with them, then my leadership would take care of me, and my troops would work harder and make sure I was also taken care of. It was a family type bond where we all help each other out. This does not apply to the civilian sector. What I have learned is people out here in the private sector are more selfish, and just do what they can to take care of themselves. Just because you took care of someone when they needed it, does not mean they will be there for you when you need them to be. I made the mistake of thinking the people I was paying to be employed by me were like family to me, and we would have each other's backs. In the end, it did not play out like this at all.

Now my expenses were close to $10,000 a month, and we were making just over that. I knew this would not be sustainable, so I imposed monthly goals for all the trainers to try to get more business in. It was not a hard goal, and most of them only needed to bring in one or two people a month or hold 4 consultations. As long as they were trying and getting people in front of me, then I couldn't hold anything against them. They found this to be difficult, and the only person who hit their goal, or made a good effort towards it was David.

On top of that my assistant was trying to come up with ways to get new business in, but it usually costs money. I spent more on advertising, or community events to let people know who we were. It was money that was not well spent. Most of her ideas did not pan out and ended up hurting the business. My head trainer and a couple of the other trainers had told me that I should just fire her because she didn't bring anything to the business and was costing us money. I did not want to do that, but looking back, I should have.

The tipping point came in January. Which is sad, because I had just asked Amanda to marry me. I had planned for 2017 to be a perfect year. The business was going to grow, we were going to get a new location, and I would be able to work less and spend more time with Amanda and my daughter. We had planned on looking for houses. My head trainer and her husband were at the dinner when I proposed to Amanda. They were good friends and knew we had all these plans, which is why when she did what she did it hurt so much more. January is supposed to be a good month for gyms and personal trainers. Everyone wants to work out and lose weight. We should have killed it, and in fact,

I signed 6 new clients. My staff did not sign anyone, except my head trainer signing one. I had told her that it is no longer her job to sign clients but to mentor the other trainers to sign clients.

In January, we barely made $5,000. My expenses did not drop though and were still close to $10,000. We took a loss. I would have been able to sustain this loss if it didn't come at a time when I was switching payroll systems. The payroll system I moved to did not cut the checks direct deposit to my employee's accounts, but it did draft the money from my account. My people were not paid on time, and I needed to pay them, so I wrote them all checks for the same amount that was drafted from payroll from my bank account. This caused my bank to flag my account for suspicious activity and freeze the rest of my assets causing a couple of checks to bounce. I then got hit with fees, and so did my employees. I was still waiting on the payroll company to refund me because I was going to go back and use the old one I was using, even though it was more expensive. It just worked much better. During this time some other business bills came due, and could not be drafted, so I got hit with more fees. I called my bank and fixed the problem, but the damage was done. I now owed a lot of money to my people and a couple of companies. I paid what I could at the time and asked my head trainer if she would take $2,000 for now and I would get her the rest when everything was sorted out. She agreed.

That should have been the end of our crisis, and everything should have gone back to normal. In fact, the beginning of February actually started out good. We made $5,000 in the first week which allowed me to catch up on some stuff, and I felt like everything would be ok. Instead of writing a check to my head trainer I did a wire transfer to her bank to be sure that the money went through. I did it on a Friday night though, so it did not process her bank until Monday. This made her husband mad. What went down essentially was caused by his ignorance and the fact that he is a coward. He should have come to me if he had a problem with the way things were but instead he went to my fiancé and stressed her out while she was at work. Her job is very demanding, and she deals with enough stress, so this caused her to panic, and she called me in tears with what he, and his wife were saying to her. I got defensive of her and went off on them. He thought I was disrespectful, but in fact, it was him who was disrespectful in the first place going to my fiancé about business stuff when he should have come to me or stayed out of it all together. He said things to her like "My wife is at home rolling quarters so we could afford to eat and buy diapers." I had told him that if he truly needed help both, myself and Amanda would have helped them out, and they were a bit dramatic. It's as if something bad had never happened to them before, so they didn't know how to handle it. It was pathetic.

Now for the even more pathetic part. As soon as the wire transfer went through I got a text message from my head trainer saying she quit. She didn't come and talk to me or try to work anything out. She didn't put in two weeks or give me any notice. She just quit. I was driving and had planned to call her when I got to where I was going to talk it out. Before I could do that, I began to get multiple emails from clients saying they wanted to discontinue their service with me. It turns out that she went behind my back and told a bunch of clients that I had not been paying her, which was a lie because I had paid her, just not what she wanted, and it was only for that one month, but she made it sound like it was the entire time she worked for me. I needed to seek legal counsel as to what I should do next. She went to train out of another gym and took a lot of my clients with her under a lie.

Just before that happened I had fired another trainer (the one my assistant recommended) because she was unreliable, the clients didn't like her, and she brought her son to work regularly and would spend more time chasing him around then training the client. So now I was down two trainers and lost a lot of revenue because she did this right before a billing cycle. This also caused some people who she sold year memberships to request a refund. It is in the contract that there are no refunds and I told them that I would continue training them. One client took it upon themselves to dispute the charge with their credit card company, even though she had already been training for months. They refunded her the full amount and hit my merchant processor with a $1500 chargeback. That caused me to not be able to get paid by the clients I did have left unless it was by cash or check.

Here is why this hurt so much. When I first hired my friend, I planned on giving her $10 an hour with commission for new clients. She was not ok with this and asked for more. I also did not plan to go through payroll but pay her as a contractor. She was worried about taxes. I spent more money to put her on the payroll as an employee and pay extra taxes. I paid her more money than she was worth because she was a friend and I wanted to take care of her, and even gave her $3,000 a month when she went full time. She ended up cutting her own hours as we hired more people and giving her clients away to our other trainers. She was salary, so it didn't matter how many hours she worked, and I think she figured that out. She began to take Mondays off and only work half days on Wednesday and Friday. She said it was because of child care, but it caused me to work even more and still pay her the same amount. I had a conversation with her about moving her to hourly because I wasn't going to pay for her to sit at home. She had an issue with this too. So, I said, "then just work more."

I could go on about how much I did for her and how much she screwed me over, but I won't. I gave her a platform to launch her career, and she used me for that. Typically it is me alone who puts me into dangerous situations, but this time it was a genuine team effort. I did not handle it well and probably made it worse. The consequences of her actions and accusations had caused my investors to become disinterested and back out. I now did not have a way to pay for the new location, which I only got because people said they wanted to move forward with me, and my assistant found a broker who found us the perfect location. The landlord would not be so forgiving about my situation and said I was on the hook for a half million dollars. As if I could just write him a check. Due to this, I lost everything.

The day she quit, I let my demon get the best of me. Instead of coming up with a plan I left my future to chance. I drove to Niagara Falls and went to the casino. This was a bad move because I had never been really lucky. I took out a few hundred dollars and sat at a blackjack table all night.

"What's wrong?" Asked the dealer.

"I lost my business today, and unless I win like $80,000 today, I am pretty much done," I answered.

This caused me to play risky and bet a lot. I did get up over $1000 in winnings but stayed and lost it all. When I was done, it was about 8pm, and I had a little over an hour drive home. I stood outside the casino and looked up at the sky. I thought to myself there was no way I was going to get myself out of this one, and I was tired. I was tired of losing everything and tired of working so hard to be so broke. I was tired of losing people. I was tired of life. The falls were only a couple minutes away, and I contemplated jumping over them and ending it. I now sat in my car and began to panic. I did not know what I was going to do. Then my phone rang, and it was Amanda. She asked me how I was doing and if I was coming back soon and reminded me that she loved me no matter what. With such a perfect woman by my side, how could I ever think to leave this world? I drove home and went to bed and left my problems for the morning.

I have reflected on all the negatives of this business and what it did to me, but I do want to highlight some of the positives because it was not all bad. I really enjoyed doing it, which is why I put in so many hours and tried to make it my career for the rest of my life. I tried twice and failed both times, but what I did end up doing was changing some lives for the better, and some people had changed my life for the better. I would like to tell a couple of their stories.

The first story I want to tell is of a couple who recently got married. Kevin and Wendy. Two of the most exceptional people I have ever met. Wendy came to me first but ended up initially working with my head trainer because I did not have time to fit her into my schedule. When my head trainer left, she then came to train with me. Before that though, she sent me her new husband Kevin, who wanted to get into shape. He was not terribly out of shape, but his eating habits were bad, and I knew if we corrected those and worked together three times a week he would lose weight fast, and he did. Training Kevin was always a lot of fun. He was a really nice and funny guy and someone who I eventually would call a friend. He lost over 20lbs working with me for the short time we worked together before I ended up having to close my business.

He was so dedicated to his fitness that he bought himself and Wendy a year of training. When the business went under, I felt the worse for them. That is a lot of money they spent to not get the services that I had promised them. I thought they would be mad, but instead, Kevin left me a voicemail saying I don't owe them anything, and that I changed their lives for the better, and they really appreciate me and see me as a friend. Wendy sent me a text message along the same lines as that message. This made me realize that there are still good people left in this world and they deserve to be taken care of. When I am able to, I will find some way to repay their kindness. They both put in a lot of work, and a lot of money, and if anyone should be upset about what happened, it should be them, but they were understanding. When I am feeling down, I will play the message that Kevin left me, or read Wendy's text, and know that at least I made a difference in a couple people's lives.

The next client I want to highlight is Kirsten, who lost over 30 pounds while working with us. She was always so nice and came in with a smile. She was happy to train with us and continuously told us what a difference it was making in her life. She was extremely dedicated to her fitness and bought three months of training up front. She also controlled herself when it came to her nutrition, which is why she saw such great results. I tell all my clients that it doesn't matter how hard you work out at the gym if your diet is terrible you will not get the results you want. Most people must think I'm joking because they do not listen to me, but the few that do really see results. Kirsten found a diet style that worked for her and kept with it. Every time I saw her, she was smaller and smaller, but she kept getting stronger and stronger. I was really proud of her. She also had a heart of gold. When she found out about the trouble, the business was having she tried to offer ways to fix it, including telling me she would pay more for our services, and a lot of people would be willing to pay more. I never wanted to raise my prices because I liked to provide the best service we could for an affordable price for everyone. Not everyone was able to afford a personal trainer, so I wanted to find a way to make it available to everyone, and I think we did a good job of that. Sure, I could have made more money if I charged more, but then I would be helping fewer people, and my real passion is helping others.

I had so many great clients that I could talk about, and not just training clients. Some of the clients I met through the program that I ran nutrition for were equally amazing, like Theresa who lost a ton of weight and is now very healthy. She had some medical problems that seem to be getting better with her health. I was so proud of her, and the dedication she showed. She was probably the only person in that program who listened to my advice 100%, and she got the best results. I wish I had time to highlight the accomplishments of all my great clients. Some of them became close to me, and I was lucky enough to call them friends. Some of them dropped out of contact with me after everything fell apart, which I understand because I was hard to reach and shut myself off from the world. There are many of them that I miss having the meaningful conversations we would have.

I met so many great people through this journey that I cannot call it a complete loss. It was not truly a failure because I had learned so much, and when I make my return to the world I will use what I have learned for the greater good of not only myself but those who choose to be around me. I do now understand the importance of balance, and what it means to "fill my cup" first, so I have the energy and resources to give to others. Otherwise, I will end up like I am now, with nothing. When you have nothing for yourself, then you have nothing to give, so it is important to take care of yourself first. I had always thought it was the other way around. If I took care of others first, then the universe or other people would take care of me because I was doing some good in the world. That is not how the real world works. It is not selfish to make sure you are taken care of. It is essential to be healthy in all aspects of your life. You need to have your physical, mental, financial, and spiritual health to be a truly successful and happy human being. These are things I am working on now.

There are some other valuable lessons I had learned from this experience. In business, you need to have a surplus of money in case you run into some hard months. At first, I had that, but I ended up spending it on employees and advertising. My hope was this would draw in new clientele, and we would build the surplus up again quickly. Do not put too much control or power into an employee who isn't ready for it. I should have never given all the responsibility I did to my head trainer. It was overwhelming, and I think it ended up burning her out. She was stressed, and I didn't see it because I was dealing with my own stress. Listen to your gut. If you have a bad feeling about someone, you are probably right. I knew my assistant was a bad person. She has a husband who she cheats on all the time with her boyfriend, and she has even cheated on her boyfriend recently with my old business partner. Her abilities as an assistant and Marketer should not outweigh her morality as a person. If she is willing to hurt the people who care about her most, then she will certainly be willing to hurt me or my business. I should have let her go a long time ago. It is important to delegate but to delegate appropriately and follow up on the tasks given until you are sure of the capabilities of your employees.

On top of what I learned about business through all of this, I also learned what I am personally capable of. I am capable of working a lot of hours with little rest. Waking up at 4am, and sometimes working until 10pm. I am capable of more physically than I ever thought I could do before, often hitting personal records on my lifts even though I was tired and run down. I am capable of learning a lot of new things on my own and implementing them in practice. I taught myself a lot through this process with research and trial and error. I also learned that I am capable of sacrificing a lot in the name of helping others. This is a good quality to have but also if left unchecked can lead to a life of misery. I learned a lot of things the hard way, but they are still good life lessons that I will take with me as I move forward.

The days following my head trainer's "resignation," led to the start of me losing my mind, again. This was the start of a domino effect that would ultimately end my business. I don't believe it was the first domino piece to fall, but it was the biggest. I believed that we could do anything if we just stuck together. We could have figured it all out. The start of all this was the paycheck mix up which caused me to get behind and not recover until February. Then when it looked like we were going to recover, she left and took almost half my revenue with her. That left me in a hard spot that I needed to improve from quick if I was going to keep things running. I went about it in the wrong way.

What was I going to do? I had no answers and no plans. I began to apply for business loans and private equity offerings. I thought that maybe a company could raise the money for me, but they were not able to. Even if they did, I felt like it was too little too late. My rent was coming due for the new location at the beginning of March. Due to what happened in February, the owner of the gym I currently worked out of was really cool with me and only charged me $300 for the month, instead of the $900 I should have paid him for my other trainers. This would help a little, but not much. I made sure I was able to pay David, as he worked really hard for me while we were going through all this. He even offered to work for free a few times. He was very understanding and truly loved what he did, so he wasn't in it for the money. He is a trainer for all the right reasons, which is why I hope he becomes successful at it.

My intern and her husband, who recently became certified and started working for me were away on vacation, so we were short, and it would cause me to work more hours than usual, which was hard to do because there weren't many more hours available. It took away from my time to solve this problem, and as I trained more and more people, I realized that each time could be the last time I trained them. What was I going to do? How would I explain this to all my clients? What was going to happen next? What about the debts that I have? I had no backup plan. These questions would stir around in my head day and night, making it near impossible to concentrate on anything else. I always believed that any problem could be outworked. Sometimes that is not the case. Sometimes you are stuck in a checkmate situation, and when you are, the sooner you realize it, the less damage will be done. There will still be damage, but you need to try to limit it with the self-realization that you have done everything you could, and now it was time to step away. I was not there yet. I was stubborn and a fighter and wanted to keep working on trying to solve the problem.

I would stay up late, or not sleep at all, writing in my notebook. Numbers, math, questions, answers. Not good answers. I would write the problems and possible solutions and then throw them away because they would not work. With each piece of paper I threw away I felt myself letting everyone down. This weighed heavy on me. I did not want to fail them. This notion of pleasing other people had caused me to abandon myself, or the people who genuinely love me, time and time again. I could not recognize that at the time. There was only the business, my employees, and the clients. I needed to take care of them. I needed to take care of the minor investors that I had, but how? I was out of time, I was out of money, and I was out of options, but I kept training people. I had not really gotten paid in over 6 months, so I was used to working for free, but my employees would not want to do that. It was the beginning of March now, and I needed to pay the gym owner and the Landlord over at the new location. I owed about $10,000.

I checked my bank account, mainly as a joke. My personal account was negative, and the business account only had a couple hundred bucks left in it. My car loan was past due, my car insurance had lapsed because I spent everything I had on paying what I could to my employees and the business to keep it running. I thought about restructuring the business and making everyone pay their own rent, but their clients would pay them directly, which would give them the opportunity to make more money in the long run. I also looked at another small location that would cost a total of $2,000 a month fully outfitted with great equipment. I thought that maybe that would be something we could all go in on together.

I planned to have a meeting in that location to go over everything with everyone and try to restructure the business to save it. I had met David at the new place the day before to talk to him about everything, and he thought it was a good idea. He was always very supportive, and I had plans to make him my head trainer because he is dedicated and knowledgeable. Seriously, if you are in the Rochester area and looking for a great personal trainer, look up David Peters. He won't let you down.

I would spend the rest of that night locked away in my room writing down all the business numbers and writing down what each trainer would get paid by their clients if we did go into a contractor type business. A system I hated, and would never work long term. I had a good presentation put together about how the next couple months will probably be rough, but we can pull through this and make it work. I would tell them not to worry about the new location, and I will find a way to take care of that. I wanted to still be their strong leader and make them believe that everything would be ok, even if I did not think it myself.

I found out after I disappointed everyone, how much some of them looked up to me. They saw me as a mentor. I think that hurt the most. When they no longer saw me as someone to look up to and instead saw me as a failure. Before all this, they would praise me about how good I was at training and how much business sense I had at such a young age. They were impressed with me, and it felt good, even though I did not believe it myself.

The meeting would never happen. I wanted it to happen. I had every intention of going and making it happen. It was not my fault it did not happen. My brain decided it had enough and it was going to take over. That day I would learn how powerful our brains really are, and what they are capable of doing. This fascinated me and pushed me into the Major I am now going to school for, psychology.

It was mid-morning, and I was in my room going over all my notes and perfecting everything for my meeting. I became hungry and decided to go down to the kitchen to get some food. My mom's office was on the first floor of the house, and I would need to walk by it to get to the kitchen. She saw me come down and go into the kitchen. I began to heat up some food, and she came out of her office to talk to me.

"Matt, we need to talk." She said.

"Okay," I said, realizing what her tone had meant.

"When is enough, enough? When are you going to stop all this and come to the reality that you are not making the right decisions?"

"I have come to that reality. I know that I have made some bad decisions, and I am working on fixing them."

"I just don't think you have your priorities straight." She continued to press me. "You are doing things in the wrong order and need to figure your life out and take care of you."

"I know. That is what I am working on right now. I have a meeting today, and I am preparing for it. I just came down here to get something to eat."

"You can't just deflect the problem by saying you know. You have been doing this for years, and it needs to stop."

"I am telling you that you are right. I understand."

"You could also help out more around the house. Like, do the dishes. I know you are going to say you are never here, but I could use your help too. I am your mother, why are you helping out people who don't actually care about you and not your own mother."

"Are you serious? I am not hungry anymore." I said as I slammed my plate down on the table.

"See! This is what I mean." My mom yelled as I ran up the stairs.

I felt myself getting worked up. She followed me yelling. I slammed my door, and she came up to open it. I was sitting by the door, and the last thing I remember is her trying to get in, then I blacked out.

I was awake, my eyes were open, and I just sat there on the ground. My mom described it as if I had left, and there was someone different sitting there. She said it didn't even look like me. My eyes were darting around the room, and I was sweating. I did not talk, and I did not move. My brain had shut my body down. Perhaps because in the past when I felt like I was backed into a corner or being threatened, I would get violent. I no longer wanted to be violent, so instead of hurting the person who gave birth to me, my brain shut me down. It was protecting others and protecting myself from myself. I often say that my demons are trying to get out of the cage, but I won't let them out. My brain knew I don't want to be that person and decided that instead of letting the demon out to play, it would just shut down.

What happened next is what shaped my recent life. It is what caused me to decide to go back to school and do things differently than I had been my whole life. It set me on a path, which now I believe is the right path for my family and me. I had thought I hit rock bottom before, but I was mistaken. This time I was really at my lowest point. The lesson I learned is that sometimes you need to hit rock bottom, so you are back at the start and can build a foundation. After all, all buildings are constructed with the foundation first. This time I was committed to building a strong foundation, so I would never find myself in this position again. I did not think of all this while I was trapped inside my head. In fact, I did not think of anything except three little words.

PART 3
RECOVERY

Chapter 14

JUST SAY SOMETHING

Just say something. Those three words began to play over and over in my head as I started to come out of my episode. My mom was on the phone with the veteran's crisis line, and three cops were standing at the door to my room. They were informed that I own weapons and came ready to defend themselves if necessary. I have no problems with the cops, in fact, one of my best friends, Andy, is a cop. He knew the ones that came to my house, and one of them recognized me, and because they knew I was friends with Andy, and I was a veteran they took extra good care of me. One of them escorted the ambulance to the hospital to make sure I got there ok. They told him he doesn't need to, and he should just leave, but he said he wanted to make sure I was ok. Police officers, much like the military, have a strong bond with each other because they endure so much. I am very grateful for the men and women who serve their communities as members of law enforcement, and I think it is terrible the way they are portrayed in the media in our country.

They walked me out to the ambulance and then strapped me into a stretcher. They said it was for my safety, but it also could have been because I was unpredictable. I don't blame them for that. They asked me some questions, and I gave short answers. Most of the ride was silent. I did not know what to say. I did not know what to expect or what was going to happen next. I was confused as to why I was in the ambulance in the first place and what was going on. I just wanted to eat something and the next thing I knew I was on my way to the hospital with a police escort. How did that happen?

It took us about a half hour to get to the hospital because we got stuck behind a train for about 15 minutes. I could tell the paramedic was nervous around me. Not because he was scared, but because it was taking so long, and he thought he had to keep me talking or entertained, and it became awkward because I did not want to talk. I stopped talking and just gazed out the back window at the police car sitting behind us. Behind him was my Mom's car. I was not sure how I should feel towards her. Should I be mad at her for calling this in or should I thank her? Was I a danger to myself or others? Could I control my anger? Was this episode going to happen again? I am not even sure what happened this time. The feeling I got from this episode was mostly fear. I felt like I was trapped in a prison and could not move.

The best way I could describe it is like a dream where something was chasing you, or maybe you had to run towards something, but you couldn't move? No matter how hard you tried to run or escape, your legs just did not work. That is how this dissociation felt. I was trapped in a dream. Semi aware of what was going on around me but not all there. My brain was working against my body as a mode of protection. Was it for my protection or the ones around me? Was it because of the overwhelming stress I had felt for being a failure and letting so many people down? For the financial struggle I was sure to face next? How can one organ be so powerful to shut down the rest of my body without my permission? It was like I gave myself a computer virus and just crashed.

We pulled into the hospital, and they wheeled me into the emergency department. I was still strapped down, and they did not yet let me up. They asked me questions and took my vitals. I was confused as to why I was there. The nurse asked me what brought me in and I said I didn't know. The paramedic explained it to her. They wheeled me into the hall where I sat waiting, still strapped down. Finally, a security guard and a nurse came to get me. The security guard had to pat me down for safety reasons. They sat me in a chair and told me to wait. A Doctor came over to clear me medically, and then they made me take off all my clothes and hand over all my possessions, including my phone. I would lose contact with the outside world, and I was supposed to meet my staff in less than an hour. I couldn't even tell them that I wasn't going to make it. My mom ended up coming back and telling the Doctor what happened because I couldn't remember.

I was now more aware of what was going on around me and why I was there. I felt horrible. When I found out that what happens next was not up to me, I felt worse. I was moved me to an uncomfortable room that had nothing on the walls, and no bed. Just a couch and chair. It was very plain. There were no tables and no other objects in the room. The room locked from the outside, and there were large windows so they could see in. There was also a camera in the room. I felt like I was an exhibit at a zoo or maybe a circus. I was not the only person in this ward of the hospital. The room next to me had a 9-year-old little girl who tried to kill herself. This made me wonder what was going on in a 9-year-old's life that made her want to end it. I thought back to when I was 9 and would just play outside, or with my friends, and thought that nothing could have been so bad that I would want to kill myself. I felt for this girl because her home life must be really rough for her to want to do that.

There was also an elderly woman who walked up and down the hall. She had one arm bent behind her back and the other one holding it. She staggered up and down the hall, pacing for hours. She moved very slow and was the closest thing to a zombie that I had ever seen. In the first room laid another older woman who kept screaming for a snack when we first got there. I looked around at the people they had locked up in here and thought to myself "do I really belong here?" I did not think I did. A nurse came in to see how I was doing and ask me some questions. He said they had a lot of other people to see and it could be 8 to 12 hours before anyone comes to see me. It all depended on what was going on that day, and what the priorities were. I was not a high priority for them, which I guess I should be proud of.

They made me urinate in a cup for a tox screen. I had never touched a drug in my life, so I was not worried about that. Lately, my mom had been asking me if I had an addiction problem because she didn't know where all my money was going and why I was tired all the time. I kept trying to explain that I was spending it on my business and employees, and I was exhausted all the time because I worked nonstop. Who had time for drugs? When they came in and said the results were negative for any drugs it was a relief for me to know that now she knows I'm not a drug addict.

My mom told Amanda about what happened and told her not to come up to the hospital because there was nothing she could do. Amanda wanted to come up and honestly, I would have liked to see her, but I understand why she told her that. She wanted to make sure I was going to be ok first and didn't want to deal with anyone else. I told her to tell Amanda to let my employees know where I am and that I will talk to them soon. Shortly after that, my dad showed up. I didn't know my mom told him about it, so I was surprised to see him. He came in and sat on the couch next to me. He did not say a word. He only looked concerned.

We waited there for hours until a woman came in to determine my mental health. She asked me a series of questions. The usual for mental health evaluations. "Do you want to hurt yourself? Do you want to hurt others? Tell me how you feel. What caused this to happen?" I answered all of her questions. This woman would be the deciding factor if I got to go home or not. If she felt I needed treatment, they would have admitted me to the psych ward for treatment, and there was no telling how long I would need to be there. She explored my past and my diagnosis of PTSD. She came up with a conclusion as to what happened to me that day.

According to her, I felt like I was backed against a wall. I felt trapped, and it caused my brain to bring me back to the last time I felt like that. It brought me back to Afghanistan and provoked a physical response. In my mind, I was back in the fight. I was being attacked, and my body didn't know how to react. Normally it would respond with a "fight" response, but I was on medication, and in the company of people who cared about me, and I cared about them, so instead I went into a "freeze" response and shut down due to the overwhelming stress that was placed on my life as of late.

As she was talking to me, my anxiety began to rise. I was hoping she would tell me that I would be able to go home. She asked if there were weapons in the house, and I replied yes. She said we needed to get them out of the house for now. This made me feel worse. It made me feel like if something were to happen, I would be unable to defend the people that I loved. In today's world, you never know what is going to happen, and I needed to feel safe, and like I could defend myself and others. It was how I was trained. I am always prepared for the worst. My dad would go to my house first to get my weapons and take them to his house. At least that was the plan.

The woman made the determination that admitting me would be a big mistake. It would make me feel even more trapped and trigger my PTSD response. It would not help me at all so instead, we came up with a treatment plan. I was to see a psychiatrist once a week and work with the VA to keep me under control. We filled out a safety plan together and talked about what to do if another episode is triggered. She mainly spoke to my mom and told her that if I need space and walk away to not follow me or it could get worse. I think she understood that now.

The one thing I really didn't like about that place (among everything else) is the way they talked to me. They used a calm and soothing voice and spoke to me like I was slow. They tried to be nurturing because they felt like I was a danger to myself and wanted to kill myself. To be clear, at this point in my life I have no will to die. I have things that I want to accomplish, and I mainly want to make sure my daughter is going to be ok. I want her to grow up with every opportunity available, and I cannot die until I know that is provided for her. I also would not be able to leave Amanda behind. That would crush her. I need to be there for her, and for her son, because I want him to grow up with me around, so I can help guide him through life. I know all of these things to be true, and I can say them out loud to people, but people don't always believe me, which is why they wanted to take my weapons away.

We were given permission to leave. I had a safety plan, and a follow up at the VA for the following day. My dad left first and went to my house, where Amanda and my sister were waiting. My guns were locked up in a safe in my room. I had the key, so he waited for me to get there. The key was in my room. My mom said that instead of moving all of the weapons and the safe to just give my dad the key, so I couldn't get into it. I agreed to that. It was a lot easier. I went up to my room to grab the key but first hid a pistol in my room. I could not feel like I wouldn't be able to defend myself. My dad asked me if all my guns were in the safe and I told him yes. I felt terrible lying to him, but I think for my mental sanity it was important for me to know I had some type of protection in the house. I hope that he will understand that when he finds out. I am no danger to myself, or others unless the others are a danger to me or my loved ones.

The VA called my mom to follow up and set an appointment for me for 1pm. It was with a counselor named Jeremy. We sat in the waiting room, and he came out to greet us. He was a shorter man who looked to be in his mid to late 30s. He had a shaved head and seemed really laid back. He told me he was in the Air Force too. We went back to his office and began to talk.

"Okay, Matt. You are here today for a follow-up because the crisis line was called is that correct?" Jeremy said.

"Yes, sir," I answered.

"Alright so walk me through what happened leading up to the crisis line being called."

I looked at my mom and wanted her to answer because I was not entirely sure. She went over what happened, and then Jeremy looked back at me.

"Does that sound about right?" He asked.

"I think so," I answered.

"Okay. My job here is to make sure you get set up with the best treatment plan. I can get you seen by a counselor here at the VA, but that could take weeks, or we can set you up with the Vet Center, since you are a combat vet and qualify for services there. It is up to you."

I looked at him and stayed silent, as I did not know what to say.

"Or I can set both up, and you can see which one you like better. How does that sound?"

"That sounds good," I answered.

Since it would take a little time to get in to see anyone else at the VA, Jeremy set up a follow-up appointment with him for the following Friday. I went home and was unsure what to do with myself now. My phone and email had a ton of messages from clients and my employees, but I had no idea what to say to them or how to respond. I was not strong enough. I sent a message to my assistant asking her to message everyone and tell them I would be contacting them next week, but I had a personal emergency. I am not sure what she actually told them, because it was not like her to keep her mouth shut about anything. I spent the rest of the day in bed.

The next morning, I woke up at 11am. That is extremely late for me. I didn't fall asleep until 3am though so it seemed about right. I could not sleep at night now because I had so much on my mind. My mom went and got me an over the counter sleep aid. It was basically Benadryl. My mind was stronger than the drug. It did not help me fall asleep, and I would often stay up until 1 or 2am. Once I was sleeping it did help me stay asleep. I always awoke in the morning to feel groggy, and my body felt heavy. It was hard to move, so I would just lay there looking at the ceiling. I had no reason to get up anyways. I no longer had a business. I no longer had a purpose. I had made big mistakes, and they could not be undone.

After a couple days of feeling this way, I remembered that a year ago I started writing this book. I had only completed the first chapter and then got busy with my new job, and then starting up my business, so I never continued working on it. I opened up my laptop and clicked on the word file. I read the first chapter to myself and thought that this would be a good way to occupy my time. I could write about everything that happened to me so I could try to pinpoint and understand where it keeps going wrong. It became a part of my routine. I would wake up in the morning and put a pot of coffee on. I would sit in a chair in the living room with my computer on my lap and type until the battery was about to die. Usually, I would write for 3 to 4 hours at a time. The time went by so fast, and it was really therapeutic. Some chapters were harder to write than others, and when I was faced to relive certain events, it would depress me for the rest of the day. It wasn't a bad thing though because it forced me to deal with it emotionally, which I think I had avoided for so many years. The more I wrote, the more of myself I got back.

It was the Monday after my episode, and I was going to meet my staff to go over everything. We were going to meet for dinner at Core Life, which was a healthy eating place that sells expensive salads. As the day went on, I felt my anxiety build. I no longer had a car or license so I could not drive myself there. They were going to send someone to pick me up, and I would basically be trapped. Amanda and my mom told me to cancel it because if something went wrong, it would not be good. I didn't want to cancel on them because they deserved answers and a plan, but I knew that I would not be able to go out in public yet. I also knew that they were not going to understand. I decided to do a conference call instead. Everyone would call in, and we could talk. They were mad about that, but there was nothing I could do about it.

David had told me that they had some ideas and a plan they wanted to go over with me. I started the call off by showing them the financial situation of the business and that I had a way to restructure it, but I wanted to hear their ideas first. No one spoke up, and then finally David said something and basically came up with the same plan that I had, and that we had already talked about. It was at that moment I heard someone hang up. I then went over how things would work if we did it that way and how everyone would get paid. Then I heard another hang up. There were only a couple of us left on the line. I ended the call and immediately got an email from an employee saying they were resigning from my business. I then tried to call my assistant who didn't answer and ended up trying to ruin my life. I called the husband/wife trainer team, and it did not go well. I understand why they were angry, but I thought of them as good friends and told them that I needed time, but I would do my best to take care of them. They did not care. I got told how awful I was and how I ruined lives. I was getting screamed at and could feel my anxiety rise even more. I felt my ability to talk start to slip away. It was getting dark, and I was home alone, sitting in my room. They hung up with me, and my mind began to drift away.

The next couple of hours I would spend in a state of dissociation. This would be the longest I would ever be detached from my body. It was pitch black in my room, but it didn't matter because I could no longer see anyways. I don't remember if I tried to call or text anyone. I don't know if I got any calls. The next thing I remember is my mom coming into my room and finding me shaking and sweating. I was trying to come out of it. She tried talking to me. She asked me what happened. Then Amanda showed up and told her about the call. I must have told her about it. My mom had some panic attack medication just in case she ever needed it. She went to get it. "Just say something," I said in my head as I began to come out of it. She came back with the pill. "Just say something." She gave me the pill and water. I sat up a little bit. "Just say something." I took the pill and laid back down. "Just say something." I said it over and over again in my head until finally I had snapped out of it and could talk. I told her what had happened, and the medication started to kick in.

"You ruined peoples lives." These words rang in my head, as I tried to process them. It is true. I took money from people, and now had no way to pay it back. Thousands of dollars from people who could not afford to lose thousands of dollars. They invested in me because they believed I was a sure thing. I was able to make them believe in me when I did not even believe in myself. Those words are what made me go mad that night. The realization that my good intentions were just a cover for the damage I had done to so many people. I was a tornado again.

Amanda stayed with me all night. I was out of it due to the medication, and she took care of me. Two times in less than a week I was trapped inside my own mind and could not escape. It's as if I had a wall up before that protected me from going into this state and now the wall had broken down, and I was vulnerable. My brain had rewired itself to be able to trap me when I couldn't handle reality. The thing is, I hated that feeling. I did not feel in control, and every time it happened, it would scare me. I didn't know how long I would be trapped and I had no idea how to get out of it. I needed to learn how to control this or healthily cope with the world so this would not happen. Until I had it under control, I knew I could not go out in public or be around people who could trigger an episode. I stayed locked away from the world.

Every day became the same. My mom would joke with me and ask if it felt like the movie Groundhogs Day. I would wake up, come downstairs, put on a pot of coffee and sit in the same chair and type for hours. The story of my life was taking up a lot of space in my brain, and I needed to get it out. Writing it all down was the best way to do this. With every chapter, I wrote, and every day that went by I began to get more and more of myself back. I could feel the old me pushing through. I still had some bad days when I was dead to the world, and there would be no way anyone could get a hold of me, but those days became fewer and fewer.

The Friday of the last episode I had I would go back to the VA and talk to Jeremy for the last time. I sat in there and told him about what happened, and he listened and talked to me about coping mechanisms. He asked me why this time I was able to snap out of it on my own, and I told him that I was laying there for a long time, and eventually became aware of what was going on. I told him that as my mom was talking to me I would repeat the words in my head "just say something" and he told me that this was a coping mechanism. He said as I focused on the words "just say something" my brain was forced to think about those words, and not the bad situation that put me in that state, to begin with. This would allow me to snap out of the trance I had been put in. I was hoping that I would not need to use this knowledge because I did not want to be in that state again, so I would avoid situations that might put me there.

I also told Jeremy that I had set up a time to see someone at the Vet center. He asked who and I told him her name. He did not know who she was. He asked if I still wanted to keep an appointment with someone at the VA and I told him that I was going to give the Vet center a chance and I would let him know if I wanted to set something up with the VA. Dr. Barry, my mental health provider, was supposed to meet with me that day as well so he could prescribe me a sleeping medicine, but he was called out on an emergency, so we had to reschedule for the following week. I was a little upset because I was still not sleeping well, and I did not like how the over the counter pills made me feel in the morning.

When I did go back to meet with Dr. Barry, he talked to me about what was happening and wanted to prescribe me a different anti-depressant to see if it would work. He would keep me on the one I was currently taking but drop the dose and add the other one to see how I tolerated it. I had some side effects at first. I would get hot, and have a fever, and my chest would burn. I got fatigued during the day and would sleep more. The side effects went away, but this would not be a medication that I would stay on for long.

The day came for me to go to the Vet center. At this point in my life, I had really stopped taking care of myself. My hair was long and messy, so I wore a hat. My beard was getting long, and I wore sweatpants and a hoodie because I did not want to put on real clothes. I looked like a mess. I walked in and up to the desk to check in. I brought a copy of my DD214 to prove my status in the military and that I was a combat veteran. The man at the front desk said he'd tried to call me; my therapist had called in sick that day. My mom, who'd driven me there since I did not have a car or license, asked if there was someone else I could see. She did not want me to have to wait until the following week, mainly because she already knew how I felt about therapy. I was not a fan. Another woman walked out and said she had no one to see at the time, and she didn't mind taking me. She told me to come on back to her office.

Her name was Amy. She is a younger therapist, and I think she is around my age. Our first session was spent getting to know each other, so I trusted her enough to tell her things. She asked me about my life and what I did for work. I told her about the whole situation with the gym and how my life had been going lately, and she seemed blown away by how overwhelming my life had been the past few months. She asked me if I would want to work with her, since she held my first appointment or if I wanted to stick with who I was scheduled with. I never even met the other therapist, so I decided to continue my work with Amy.

One thing we talked about was developing a plan for what my life would look like now. At this point, I did not have a plan. I did not know what was going to happen to me, and I was just waiting to be sued. I knew I would have to file bankruptcy. I was waiting for the bank to come and take my car. I was pretty much just stuck waiting for things to keep getting worse and keep getting harder. When I went home that day, I really thought about what I wanted to do and how I would go on with my life moving forward. I could not just stay stuck in the spot I was in because I would never get better that way. I was cleaning my room and going through some old paperwork and found my old folder from RIT, from when I signed up the previous year. I decided to send the admission's office I was working with an email to see if they still had all my records on file. They did! I told him that I was interested in going to school in the fall and asked what I needed to do.

While I waited for a reply from them, I went on the school's website and looked at the different programs they offered. I clicked on psychology. I looked at the classes required for that degree and decided it was something that I could do. I knew it would be challenging, but that is part of what I liked about it. What would I do with this degree? The people I would train often said I was like a therapist to them because they would talk about their problems with me and I would listen. Why not actually help people with their problems? I would not want to help just anyone though. I decided I would help veterans like me since I went through everything myself and could offer some good insight and advice. Maybe I could stop a vet from making some of the same mistakes I made. Perhaps I could change their lives for the better. This was what I wanted to do with my life now. I had a new goal and a purpose again.

Chapter 15

AND HOW DOES THAT MAKE YOU FEEL?

My past experiences with therapy would leave me skeptical about going in and talking to someone again. Like most veterans and probably most men, I thought that seeking help made me look weak. What I ended up realizing is that without the support I was weak. I was in a cycle of disaster and could not break it on my own. Therapy offered me an outlet to talk about everything going on in my head and hear the perspective from an outside and educated source.

One of my favorite analogies is from a friend of mine named Morgan. She is a member of AA. She tells me that her sobriety is in a bucket, and when things happen to her during the week, she needs to use a little bit of her sobriety from the bucket. When she goes to her meetings, it is like refilling the bucket. I am not sure if this is an AA analogy or hers, but I like it because that is how I feel about meeting with Amy at the vet center. Instead of sobriety in a bucket though, mine is sanity. The world has desperately tried to empty my bucket of sanity, and I am glad I found a way to keep it full…for the most part.

When you walk into the vet center, you are welcomed by the smell of a fresh pot of coffee and some sort of baked goods on the table. Luke, behind the counter, who is a former Marine, is there to greet you and let your counselor know you have arrived. There are comfortable chairs, in the waiting room, and the radio is on. They have free wifi and reading material. Often other vets are sitting there waiting for their appointments. We span many different wars and conflicts. My favorite is talking to the old Vietnam war vets because they usually have some good insight.

While sitting in the waiting room before an appointment one day, an older black gentleman from the Vietnam war struck up a conversation with me and one other guy. The other guy looked like he had been blown up. He had terrible scars on his arms and legs, and walked with a cane, even though he was roughly my age.

"You boys in the sands?" The Vietnam vet asked.

"Yes sir" We both answered.

"That must have been terrible." He said.

"I think you probably had it worse," I said to him referencing his Vietnam Vet hat.

"Nah. We had two things over in Nam that you boys didn't have in the Sands." He said.

"What's that?" Asked the other vet.

"Beer, and pussy." He answered.

We laughed, and he turned the conversation to a more serious note.

"Do you guys still sleep in the same bed as your lady?" He asked.

"Yeah." We both answered.

"How? Aren't you worried about hurting her? I wake up so violently. I sleep in a separate room now."

"I have woken up to my girl crying before because I hit her in my sleep, or choked her on accident, but it hasn't happened in a while," I said, trying to offer him some comfort.

"Even after that, she will still sleep next to you?"

"Yes."

"She must really love you then." He said.

Amy came out from her office to get me, and I wished the man good luck as I walked with her back to her office. Sadly, this kind of thing happens to married veterans all over the country. Dealing with the side effects of PTSD or any trauma-related disorder can be very straining on a relationship, and if not handled appropriately can lead to distance between two people. That is why periodically I will bring Amanda to see Amy with me, so she can hear what I am going through, and also voice her concerns in a safe place, and we can work on them together. All relationships take work, no matter what, but with us, there is an added piece that needs to be addressed continuously or it will consume us.

In the beginning of my time with Amy, I was quiet and reluctant to open up. She would ask me questions designed to get me to talk, and I would answer them in the shortest manner possible. It helped that in the beginning, my mom came with me to fill Amy in on everything that had been going on with me. She didn't really have a choice though, because I had lost my car, and needed a ride there. She would also go to a group meeting which was meant to support the family members of people suffering from PTSD. She told me she learned a lot and it was good for her to know that what was going on with me was "normal" to an extent.

After the first three weeks, I would begin to go to my sessions alone. I started to feel more comfortable with Amy and began to share more with her. Through learning about me and my past traumas, she recommended we do a type of exposure therapy called EMDR. Basically, it is recalling traumatic events in my life that took place and working through them in a particular way. We set up a plan to begin this, but we did not start it until months later due to some events in my life that I needed to deal with first. I would still go to her each week, but we would just do our usual talk therapy, and she would listen to my concerns and help me work through them.

As I said before, we came up with a good life plan for me. I would be attending RIT to get a degree in psychology. This has been a crucial part of my healing because I crave structure and organization. Without it, I go crazy. We needed to make sure I wouldn't fall back into a pattern of mania though. I tend to get carried away and let the things I am working on consume me. I become a perfectionist and spend all my time devoted to that one thing that I am doing. I wanted to be sure I had time for my family, and time for myself, so we went over some strategies, such as setting a time limit for school work so I can be sure I had time to focus on other things. This really helped when it came to keeping me level.

One of the strange things about being a psychology major and a patient at the same time is I am able to pick up on a lot of things Amy does, that I have learned about in school. Also, I am able to have a better understanding of why I am the way that I am. For example, through studying abnormal psychology, I saw that I fit the textbook definition of having bipolar 1 disorder. Right out of the DSM 5. I have full episodes of mania, followed by full episodes of depression, and it has been going on for years. For years, I have had these problems, and they have gone undiagnosed. Now that I am aware of what the symptoms of a manic episode are, I can watch out for them and stop myself before I do something stupid and ruin my life again.

Amy is excellent when it comes to counseling me and helping me stay focused. She will even email me or call me during the week if she knows something significant has happened, just to make sure I am processing it ok. In our sessions, she will use a phrase that I have come to pick up on as one of her techniques. She will say "what would it look like if…" and then finish the sentence, giving you another perspective to see a situation from. It is a useful technique and often results in some kind of enlightening insight or a new idea.

Every week when I leave the vet center I feel like a weight has been lifted off my shoulders. I got out all the frustrations from the week and have been given some positive feedback and new ideas on how to move forward with my life. It really is like refilling my bucket with sanity. There has only ever been one time that I left that office feeling worse than when I walked in, and it was necessary for my recovery and not Amy's fault.

It was at the beginning of our EMDR sessions. The way EMDR works is you first bring up a disturbing event, and while you are talking about it, you move your eyes back and forth in a rhythmic pattern, usually following someone's finger. This is supposed to trick your brain into thinking it is in REM. You are to let your brain wonder where it wants to go, and after a few seconds, you focus on how you are feeling physically. Keeping that in mind you continue the process. Usually between 5 and 10 trials per session, or until you no longer feel bad.

When I try to explain what EMDR does, I relate it to a computer. Let's say you save a file in the wrong folder. You realize it is in the wrong folder, and now you need to move it to the right folder. Your brain is the computer, and the file is the irrational response you have to a "trigger." EMDR is the cursor moving the file. It is much more complicated than this, but if you want to boil it down to its simplest form than that is basically what it is.

Our first session of EMDR was finding my "happy place." We would call it grounding. Something I could use to come back to reality if I had gone too far. A place I could go in my head to come back in case I dissociated.

"I want you to close your eyes and picture someplace calming," Amy said.

"I will try," I said as I closed my eyes and scrambled to find a calming place.

"Do you have it?"

"Not yet."

"Okay, let me know when you do."

A couple of minutes passed, and I was able to come up with a location. I chose Niagara Falls.

"I got it."

"What did you pick?"

"Niagara Falls."

"Why did you pick there?"

"It is a place I have been many times. I went there with my brother and grandparents when I was young. I went there with my brother and friend before my brother shipped out to Basic. I went there with some recruits before bringing them to MEPS. I went there for my birthday with Amanda. Every time I go see the falls I am happy and calm."

"Perfect. Now I want you to imagine you are there right now. What do you feel?"

"I feel the mist from the falls hitting me. I smell the water. I feel the cool breeze. I feel warm inside, and safe." I said

"Great. I want you to keep this feeling in mind, and whenever you are about to have an episode, try to go to this place."

It may sound weird, but this technique really does work to calm me down when I am getting worked up. The problem is I have to know when to use it. Sometimes, it might be too late. People with PTSD or severe anxiety from trauma have what's called hypervigilance. If you look at it as a scale of 1 to 10, where a reasonable person's stress and anxiety is around a 2 or 3, a person with the disorder is always at an 8 or 9, so it does not take much to get them to a 10. This can be a problem when trying to recognize when to use a technique like grounding. Having a short fuse can be scary for the person suffering, and the people around them.

The next session we would begin EMDR with the most significant trauma. Before we started, I was asked how I felt about myself and how I wanted to feel. I told Amy that I felt like I am undeserving of happiness and love and that I wanted to feel like I deserved those things. When confronted with why I think this way, I come up with two main reasons. Reason one is that I have taken life. I have separated souls from their body, and now I don't deserve to live among the masses who have never done that. The second is all the people I have failed. With the crumbling of each business, I have let people down, hurt people, lost them money, and made it harder for them to trust in other human beings. For those sins, I am unworthy of happiness and love.

The goal was to get myself from feeling undeserving to deserving through revisiting all the traumatic experiences of my past to facilitate new learning and a new way of processing what happened. Sounds easy enough, right? It is as easy as tearing off a scab and re-exposing a wound. That is essentially what you are doing. However, I know from experience that no growth ever comes without a little pain, so I was ready to endure.

"I want to go back to that night in Afghanistan," Amy said.

"Alright."

"Are you ok with going there?"

"Yes."

"I want you to put yourself back there in your mind. What do you feel? What is happening to your body? What image describes that event?"

"Blood and sand. Not like the sand you would find at the beach. Sand might not even be the right word for it since it is hard, like dirt. It still has the capabilities of getting everywhere though."

"Blood and sand will work. What do you feel?"

"I felt my body temperature rising. I am starting to sweat, and I feel anxious." I replied.

"Now I want you to focus on those feelings and follow my finger."

She began to move her finger back and forth as I focused on the feeling and let my mind wander to where it wanted to go.

"Tell me where you went," Amy said.

"I was wondering what I was even doing there that night. The conditions all had to be perfect for this to even happen. Why did it happen to me?"

"How does that feel?"

"Confusing and sad."

"Hold those feelings and follow my finger."

Again, I focused on the pain as I followed her finger.

"What are you thinking now?" She asked.

I stayed silent for a moment before answering. I was trying to process my thoughts and feelings and form them into words.

It was hard to do, and I wondered if I was slipping away again. I fought with myself to say anything. Then the words came out.

"They were unarmed. I didn't have to kill them. I probably had to shoot them, but I didn't have to kill them."

"How do you feel right now with those thoughts?"

"Like a monster. A murderer. Damned. Like I don't deserve anything."

We went a few more rounds, and where people usually improve, I just got worse. It became clear to Amy that I was going to need more time, but unfortunately, we were out of time. She tried to ground me, but that only worked for a moment. I went out to my car, and sat there for a minute, trying to bring myself back to reality. I would be unsuccessful. Its as if I just willingly let the demon out to play, and I did not have the location of the cage anymore. This would be a hard week for me.

I fought with Amanda, way worse than anything ever before. I broke things and tried to leave. She was pregnant at the time, and me stressing her out was dangerous for her and our baby. I saw her break down and fall to the ground as I put my coat on. This made me stop. For the first time ever, I had seen Amanda cry out of pain, and out of love. I have seen Amanda cry many times before, because she is very sensitive, and will cry when things are happy, and when TV shows or movies are sad. I had never seen her like this. Suddenly I hated myself all over again. I put my coat back in the closet and went upstairs to cool off. She sat on the ground with our dog, Gambit.

When she finally came up, I told her that I loved her, and I would never leave her. I said I was sorry, and I needed to do better. I explained what I was doing in therapy and how it made me feel that week. It was not just at home either. It was in school as well. I could not concentrate and left school early almost every day that week. I wanted the demon back in the cage, and Amy was the only one who could help me.

I went back to her office for our next appointment and told her what was going on. She had a feeling it was going to be a hard week for me, and we jumped right into EMDR. This session was much more successful, and I was able to lock away that side of me, and even feel better about myself. Since then, I have had almost no anxiety when thinking about that event. It is a memory now that does not elicit a physical response. I would not say I am cured, because we have not yet worked through every part of it, or what happened with my businesses, but that is partially my fault.

After I felt better, I was scared to do EMDR again, because I wasn't sure which one of us would be leaving Amy's office that day. So, since I have been feeling good, I found ways to avoid EMDR and come up with excuses as to why we can't do it every week. I know that I am going to have to do it at some point, and I am looking forward to the end result, just not the road to get there. As I know, nothing worth having comes easy.

Chapter 16

THE TRAIN AND THE TRACK

One thing I tell some of the younger students at RIT is it is great to have a plan but be flexible. Talking from experience, I have never had a plan that worked out the way I had intended it to. I am sure some people do, but I bet most people must come up with another plan along the way. The plan that Amy and I developed for my life was no different. There would be temptations, and distractions, and unexpected events that would try to derail my plans. One of our main objectives in therapy was to keep me on track.

The month was July 2017, and my brother was about to get out of the Air Force. At the time I was still living at my moms, but Amanda had just bought a house that was closing in August, and I was going to be moving soon. I stayed a week at my friend Andy's house to watch his dog while he was out of town, and then I planned to go from there to the Airport to fly to Barksdale Air Force Base, to help my brother move back to NY.

I needed to grab a few things from home before I left for Barksdale. I walked in the door, and my mom was in the kitchen. She asked me if I wanted something to eat. I told her no, and I was just going to pick up a couple of things that I need before I went to get Nick. The conversation then turned towards Amanda and her new house, since my mom was helping her with her closing, and did all her paperwork.

"Is Amanda excited to move into her new house?" She asked

"Yes, she can't wait."

"So, what are your plans? Do you still want to move in with her?"

"That's the plan," I said.

"I just don't think it's a good idea right now. You should stay here with me for a little while longer until you get on your feet. You are starting to get much better, but you are still not all the way there."

"We have had this talk before, and I will be fine."

"You always say that, and every time you haven't listened to me you have not been fine, and then I am left to help you clean up the mess."

"Okay, but now I am getting help, and have a plan, and everything will be okay."

"What if you get better and realize you don't want to be with her anymore because you are a different person when you are better?"

"That isn't going to happen. No offense but you are the last person I should take relationship advice from. You have been divorced twice, and your current relationship is like a high school one. You break up all the time, and then get back together."

This apparently offended her, as it should have. For the record, I like her boyfriend. He is a good guy and treats her well. I was just angry at the time and said whatever I could to make her stop. She was just trying to help me see the situation clearly, and I was in the wrong for how I reacted.

"Watch the way you talk to me." She said.

My blood began to boil, and this would have been an excellent time to go to my happy place, but I didn't think of that. She said something that upset me even more, and I slammed my fist into the table. She screamed at me to get out of her house. At that moment I got up and stood in front of her.

"Go ahead, hit me. Kill your mother!" she said, "I know you hate me, but you know what, I hate you too."

I had never once said I hated my mom, and I don't. To hear her say that to me was shocking. I turned around and went to leave. She started to push me. I kept it together as I headed for the door.

"Leave and never come back!"

"Don't worry, I won't," I said.

Here is the problem. I did not get anything I needed for my trip, and I didn't have a car, so I just started walking. I tried to call Amanda, but she didn't answer. Then my phone decided to freeze and turn itself off in my pocket. I walked a few miles to the mall and just sat in the parking lot. Eventually getting a hold of Amanda, she came and picked me up and took me back to Andy's. I told her everything that happened.

She called my mom to see if I could come to get my stuff, and she said no, but Amanda could go and pick it up. I wanted to go to make sure I got everything, but I didn't have a choice, so Amanda went and picked up what I needed. I figured anything I was missing I could just buy once I got to Barksdale. Amanda spent the night with me at Andy's since she was going to be dropping me off at the Airport in the morning.

At the Airport we said goodbye. I would miss her, but I would only be gone for a few days. I made my way through security and to my gate. The trip there was rather uneventful, and it gave me time to think about what had happened. I needed to find a place to stay for two weeks while I waited for the house to be ready. I wasn't sure what I was going to do, but I decided to wait until the drive back to figure it out since I would have a lot of time to think, and my brother to help me out.

I landed at the Shreveport Airport, where my brother met me. I had not seen him for some time, so it was nice to be reunited. Since the last time I saw him, his wife and he had split up, and he was taking it kind of hard. I think the timing of his coming home was perfect because he would need his friends and family now more than ever.

"Hey! How was your flight?" Nick said as we hugged hello.

"Not bad. I forgot how hot it is here."

"Yeah, especially in July. Do you have any luggage you need to get?"

"Yes. So how are you holding up?"

"Not to bad. Everything is basically packed up and ready to go. The movers should be coming tomorrow to get it."

"Awesome. Then we can get out of here."

I grabbed my luggage and went to Nick's car. We drove to the base, and he talked about all the things that had been going on with him and his wife. It was sad to me because he had followed in my footsteps and now would be getting divorced. Maybe it is genetic. We must have a divorce gene that makes us get divorced at least once. Hopefully we both won't have to go through that again.

We got to his house and went inside. I had been there before only now it looked much different. What was once full of life made together by two people was now empty. Boxes sat where the dining room was. Most of the house now empty except for a couch, TV and a bed. It was sad that this is how his chapter in the Air Force had ended. I was glad, however, to have my brother back.

"I got us some steaks. Ribeye." Nick said.

"Sweet. Let's fire up the grill."

"Want a beer?"

"Yeah."

"So, mom called me."

"Oh yeah? She went a little crazy."

"Maybe. I am not taking sides. I just don't think it's a good idea for you guys to live together."

"I know that. I was moving in a couple weeks. I start school next month too. She is on me about things, but what does she want me to do? It's not like I can get a full-time job right now with starting school in a month, and I tried to get a part-time job at GNC, but they wouldn't hire me because they wanted my class schedule first. So, I am stuck in limbo for another month."

"I know Matt. It will all be okay."

We ate our steaks and continued to drink. We then decided to play some video games, and just hang out like old times. Amanda was texting me and asked if there were any good strip clubs around. I said I wasn't sure, and it didn't matter because we wouldn't be going to any. I never liked them. They didn't make sense to me. Why throw money away just to see a girl dance naked. At the time she asked me if we were going out to a strip club we were watching a person play a video game on Twitch. I know. We were pretty cool.

The next day a person from the moving company came to take inventory. Nick had to go in for his final out processing, so I stayed at the house with her while she opened all the boxes and wrote down everything that was packed up. She labeled everything and was about to leave when I asked her what time the movers were coming. She said she didn't know, and it would probably be a couple of days. This was not the plan, and Nick did not know that. When he came home, he was already in a bad mood. He had not done anything on his out-processing checklist. He didn't even know he had one. He said they never gave it to him and how was he supposed to know. I picked up a folder from the counter that said out-processing, pulled out the checklist from it and showed it to him. He stopped his rage and just laughed.

"You better get working on this," I said

"Yeah, I will be back."

He left again and now I was alone. I don't blame him for not finding the checklist. He had a lot going on. He had to pack up his whole house alone, which was probably a constant reminder that his wife was not there. Going through that with her obviously took a toll on him mentally, and that was to be expected.

Nick finished his entire out-processing checklist in one day, which is extremely impressive. He called to see when the movers were coming, and they would be to his house the following day between 8 and 10, but we would need to go to the gate to let them on base. We waited for a while and called them again. They were running behind. We wanted to leave, and we needed to have the keys to the housing office by 1pm, or we would have to wait another day. The movers finally arrived around 10, which gave us only a couple hours to get everything packed up and get to the housing office. They sent two guys. One of the guys was very small and looked like he had never moved anything in his life. The other guy was bigger, but it looked like he was in charge, and was writing down all the ID tags and what was in the boxes on a sheet of paper, leaving all the moving to the other guy.

"We are never going to get out of here," I said to Nick.

"You are right. Not if we let them move all this. Let's start loading the truck."

We began to move everything that had been tagged by the one guy writing everything down. The smaller gentlemen would tell us where to place the items in the truck. They watched us work, and did very little to help us out, which was fine because between Nick and myself we have moved over a dozen times and were basically pros at it by now. We finished around 12:30pm, and Nick ran the keys over to the housing office. We were now ready to start our 18-hour drive back to Rochester NY.

I have done this type of drive on 4 different occasions. To and from Texas, and to and from Arizona. This time went by the fastest. I think it was because I was in no hurry to get home. I still did not know where I was going to stay. On the trip home I called Andy, whose house and Dog I had watched before going to get Nick and asked him if I could crash on his couch for a couple of weeks until the closing date of Amanda's house. Andy has always been a good friend and is one of the most dependable people I know. He told me I could stay there as long as I needed.

Nick was moving into Andy's house and taking one of his spare rooms. He also had another guy, Curran, living there. With the four of us living there it was like a frat house. This wasn't always a good thing if I wanted to sleep and the boys were up until 4am drinking and playing ping pong in the basement. For the most part, though, it was enjoyable. We would wake up in the morning and Nick, Curran, and I would go to the gym for a couple hours. We then would go home and either work in Andy's backyard chopping down trees or hang out in the house and play games. I was working on writing articles and managing a web page to keep me busy during the days. Mostly though we just had fun. It had been a while since I had fun with the guys and it was nice to bond with them again and to have my brother home.

Dinner time was like a ritual. We would usually pick up some meat to grill and a 12 pack of beer. I would be outside on the grill, since they decided I was the best at it and Curran would be inside making the sides. Nick would help out were needed, and usually did most of the cleaning up afterward. Andy owned the house and is a cop who works through the night, so we made sure he did nothing but enjoy the meal, and usually made extra for him to take to work.

Towards the end of my time there I began to feel worthless. Amanda had been working hard at a job she hated so she could save up for a house, and I was not able to help her at all. I had lost everything, and the money I was getting now was going to bills and debts. I never had any left over for her or for me. Soon I would be moving in with her and did not want her to take care of me. It should be the other way around. I just felt like a loser, and like everyone else saw me that way too.

The guys wanted to watch a movie one night, but first, we went to the liquor store. We each got what we wanted. I grabbed a handle of Jack Fire (which is basically Jack Daniels version of fireball) and a bottle of wine. I had not intended on finishing it all that night…or maybe I did. I can't really remember, because I did drink all of it. It was a lot of alcohol to take in so quickly. I remember we started watching "John Wick 2", and I began to drink. I was using the wine as a chaser for the Jack I drank straight from the bottle. Before the end of the movie, both bottles were gone. There must have been something about Keanu Reeves calm demeanor while he was destroying people that made me feel invincible. I don't remember most of the movie and couldn't tell you how it ended.

I crossed the threshold from a happy drunk to the room is spinning and needed to lie down. The room would not stop spinning, and now I felt sick.

"Hey, Andy!" I called out.

"Yeah, Matt?"

"Can you help me up?"

"Are you going to throw up?"

"weeeellllllll, maybe."

"Okay, I will get you to the bathroom."

Andy helped me to the bathroom. I almost didn't make it and felt it coming up right before I got there. I ran the rest of the way and started right before the toilet. I hit the back of the toilet, but really didn't make too much of a mess. At this point, Andy went to get Nick, who would take over from here. Nick called Amanda, and she came over after work to take care of me. I was still out of it.

We were laying on the couch trying to sleep. Amanda rubbing my head and asked me what I was thinking.

"Why do you want to be with me?" I asked.

"I love you, what do you mean?"

"Why. Lately, I have been nothing but a burden to you."

"That's not true. You make me happy. You are just going through a rough time, and I would never leave you."

"I promise I will make all this up to you. I love you."

I passed out not too long after that. The next morning the hangover wasn't as bad as I expected it to be. I think it was because Amanda kept making me drink water. She was good when it came to taking care of people. That is why she is the best nurse out there.

We moved into our new house only a week before school started. The month of August flew by, and I was so busy I did not have time to get into my head. I was still nervous about starting school. I had been out of school for 12 years and hoped it wasn't hard to get back into the swing of things. I adapted pretty quick. I think the structure and deadlines were good for me. It allowed me to create a schedule for myself that I could follow and stay motivated. I worked really hard and found that I was still very good at school. Realizing this solidified that this was where I was supposed to be.

Before this, I was sent continuously e-mails about opportunities or jobs. Some of them looked really good, but I had to force myself to ignore them. I did not even inquire for more information because I knew if I went down that road all the progress I had made would be undone, and I would not go to school. I needed to follow this path, not only because it was a smart path to follow, but also to prove to myself that I could. To prove that I could avoid distractions and follow through with a plan that will set me up for the rest of my life.

This was not always easy for me, and the temptations were everywhere. I was lucky though because I had a good support system. I now lived with Amanda who could keep me on track and went to see Amy every week whose job it was to make sure I was sticking to the plan. She would regularly check up on me and ask me how things were going and if I was sticking to the path that we had laid out. Anytime I got an idea about something else I could be doing along with school she would tell me to remember my past habits and ask if I thought that was a good idea. It never would have been a good idea. It would have led to another manic episode and the destruction of my life as I know it.

Earlier I equated my life to a video game and losing lives and having to start all over. At this point, I didn't think I had any lives left. If I messed up where my life was going now, then I was pretty sure the damage would be irreversible. I know that most people will tell you there is always a way out, and you can come back from anything, but the problem is I know I wouldn't want to. I needed this to work, and I needed my life to never fall apart again. I am not talking about everyday life problems.

Those I can handle calmly and with ration. I am talking about a full implosion of my life. Where I lose the girl, the house, the school, everything I have worked for. This is what the demon will try to take from me, and this is what I must fight every day to keep.

Chapter 17

THIS LITTLE LIGHT OF MINE

Darkness. The absence of light. That is what life is if you do not let the light in. It becomes easy and addicting to isolate yourself from the world. Sit alone in your room without a care, and without those who care. It will make you go crazy. You cannot truly find yourself until you find your place in the world, and it is not to be alone. You were made for something more. You grew from a single cell into a fully functional human being in 9 months. Your brain is constantly learning and adapting to the environments, sending signals faster than you can fathom all over your body. You are an extraordinary miracle of nature, and you need to let the light in.

This took me many years to figure out. I returned from Afghanistan in 2007 but did not seek help until 2014 (with medication only). I spent 7 years in the dark. 7 years with just my thoughts. 7 years with the demon being the only thing I could really talk to. The only thing who knew what I really was and what I had done. I shut the world out for 7 years. I thought that is what I had to do. I accepted it as fact that this was the life I was going to live until I die. I was stuck in a monotonous cycle of daily darkness I could not escape.

When I finally did get help, both times, it was not of my own free will. The first time I was found by my father, and the second time I was taken by Ambulance to the hospital. Wouldn't it be so much easier to just go of your own free will? To not have the ones you love suffer the worst parts of you. I wish I had done things differently, but I can't go back and change it. I can only move forward, and recognize where I struggle, and when to ask for help. It is not weakness to ask for help. It is a strength to bond together with other human beings to achieve a common goal. Avoidance brings pain, which can be debilitating, and then you will know weakness. All alone you will sit in your room for days, accomplishing nothing. That is true weakness.

I found good news out of all this though. The person who sits here today is not who you are, but who you were. It is the result of all your past choices. You can make the decision today to do something different and become something different. Use your time to grow and strengthen, and you will know happiness. That is what I am doing, and it is a process. Not every day has been good, and I know that I will have more bad days in the future. The good days and the end result makes the bad days tolerable. Without the bad days, we would not know what the good ones look like, and we may let them pass us by. Don't shy away from the challenge but embrace it. It will shape you into who you want to be. Who you are meant to be.

Today I have straight A's at an excellent school that I get to attend for free thanks to my service to my country. I am studying a topic I am passionate about and am on the Dean's list. Psychology has taught me so much about myself and others already, and I am eager to get out there and help more people. I am eager, but patient and know it will take time. My goal is to get a Ph.D. in Clinical Psychology and help as many of my brothers and sisters as I can. I would also like to go into research and see if I can find a solution more meaningful than any that have been found before. I want to leave a lasting impression on this world that even the one's once broken can be repaired stronger than ever.

We are continually upgrading our house. The projects are fun for me, and I love turning this old beat up house into a home for our children and us. My son is due June 14th, 2018, and we are preparing for his arrival. I can't wait to meet him. I found the perfect woman for me who I know will stand by my side through anything. She deserves so much, and I will continue to do my best to give it to her.

She is everything I have ever needed. She is the most supportive person I have ever met. Everything about her is rare. From her look, down to her heart. There is no one on this planet like her. She has platinum blonde hair and stands out in a crowd. It is as bright as her personality. Her light-colored eyes can capture the attention of any man. You would not be wrong to compare her to a Disney princess. In fact, a little girl once when we were out couldn't stop staring at her. Her mother looked at Amanda and said, "I'm sorry, she thinks you look like a princess." I looked at the little girl and quietly said: "she is." The girl smiled shyly. That is Amanda though. She brings joy anywhere she goes. The darkest room will light up brighter than the sun when she walks in. All people and animals love her because she is genuine and kind. She would not hurt a soul, even if they deserved it. She saves spiders and puts them outside. Who does that? A person that genuinely cares for all life. That is why she is fantastic at being a nurse. Everyone she cares for in her profession is lucky to have her. I will never forget how lucky I am to have her by my side.

Her son Sean has her heart. He cares about people the way she does and is such a sweet boy. For that reason, I love him like a son. I wish I got to spend every day with him and Morgan. My daughter adores him, and he adores her. He wants to go anywhere and do anything she does. He looks up to her. He is still a boy though, so when it comes to doing boy things like throwing or kicking a ball around, that's where I like to play with him. Right now, he is only 4, but he has such an athletic gift. He can throw a ball better than most kids twice his age and can hit a golf ball with a near perfect swing already. He is also brilliant for his age. He was born 3 months early and almost didn't make it. He fought through and survived, and I think because of that he is very gifted. He is an exceptional boy who is a fighter and can survive anything. I can't wait to watch him grow up into an incredible man.

Morgan loves Amanda too and is excited to have her for a stepmom. Amanda is great with her. She plays dolls with her, and has tea parties, and pretty much does whatever Morgan wants her to do. Amanda loves to play all the girly games with her because she has a boy and doesn't get to with him. I am not as good at tea parties as her, so Morgan prefers to play with her, but that's ok because I can do boy stuff with Sean, so it all balances out. When the four of us are together, its perfect. It's my idea of an ideal family, and that is all I want, and all I need to be happy. I just want to make sure I have a way to take care of them. That is one of the reasons I worked so hard. I wanted to provide a comfortable life for all of them, so they never had to worry about money, or had to sacrifice like I had too.

Amanda has bailed me out more times than I can count. It's sad when I think about it. Trying to run a successful business had negatively impacted her. When I spent all my money on the business and needed some for gas, she would give me gas money. When my car got repossessed, she paid to get it back. She has been there for me time and time again, so when I can spoil her, I do. One year for her Birthday I surprised her and took her to Lake George. We went to six flags, so she could feel like a kid again because she was worried about getting older. I took her horseback riding because Horses are her favorite animal, and she rode competitively as a child. I wanted to make sure she had the best birthday ever because she deserves the best. I don't feel like I am the best, and I know she could do better, so I am grateful for how much she loves me. Her beauty could attract any guy in the world, and her heart would keep them.

Wherever she walks, there is life. Flowers bloom around her as if they can sense her magic. She truly is sent by God to make this world a better place. How fitting is it that she is a nurse. She works exclusively with the elderly, and many times they pass away where she works. It is basically hospice care. I say they are lucky, that the last thing they see is her and when they open their eyes again they are in heaven. She is the Angel that brings them to their final resting place. The last thing they see on Earth is the best Earth has to offer. God has placed her here for a purpose, and I believe she is in my life for a purpose too. She has saved me and continues to do so. I am hoping to become the man she deserves and repay the world for giving her to me. I need to do great things with my life because she has given me a chance too.

Before her, I never knew what true love was. She has shown me how to love, and what it should look like. Most people say they have a guardian Angel in heaven, mine came to Earth to be by my side when I needed her the most. I wish the world had more people like her. Then it would be a better place. Sadly, I have only ever found one. She is one of a kind.

My mother and I made up around the time my little sister left for Basic training. Our relationship is better now, and I talk to her every week. My sister is stationed in NC as a Cyber Systems Operator. It was not her first choice, and she thinks its boring, but she will thank me when she gets out and can get a six-figure job right away.

My brother seems really happy now. He is working for a local Fire Department, and part-time at a gym, where he spends most of his day anyway, so he might as well get paid for it. It is nice to be able to see him whenever I want and have him so close again. I am really proud of everything he has accomplished and know he will continue to have a great life. The life I want for him and for my sister. I just hope her time in the Air Force is more relaxed than mine, and she has great experiences and avoids the mistakes I made.

Morgan is eleven now and in sixth grade. She gets good grades and despite her rocky upbringing has an amazing heart. I could not ask for a better daughter. Her mother, Alyssa, and I get along pretty well now. We don't fight anymore and do what we have to when it comes to our daughter's happiness and well-being.

The people I was close with when I owned my businesses have all left me. I can no longer do anything to benefit them, so our friendship ended. This hurt the most because I felt used. Some of them had a good reason to hate me, so I don't blame them for that. Most of them turned on me because of lies spread by my old assistant, who loved drama. People are welcome to think what they like, but I do regret losing some of those people as friends.

The realizations I have made through this whole process are what keeps me moving forward. I have recognized that I have a problem. I recognized that I have a cycle that I keep falling into. I now can recognize those patterns and stop it before it is too late. I realized I needed help and could not get better on my own. It was not when I was forced to go there, but after that, I made the decision for myself. When I saw that it actually was helping me, it reinforced my ability to recognize the role therapy plays in the healing process. I am happy that I realized all of this before it was too late. If I continued on my path uninterrupted, I might not be here today.

The problem with illnesses like depression, and anxiety, is they are often hard to recognize in others. Some people are very good at hiding it. They can appear to live a happy and healthy life to those around them, and then go home to be surrounded by darkness and fear. Much like my professional life, which always seemed like I had it together, when in fact I was suffering a lot behind the scenes.

22 Veterans commit suicide a day. There are many reasons why. We need to work together to get this number down to 0. No one should ever feel like they no longer have a place in this world. It is a large goal, but an important one. We need to do a better job of recognizing those who need help and providing it. Those who have the same issues I have need to do a better job reaching out for help. I know that it is hard, but it is the right thing to do, and there are people that care. The responsibility is on all of us. The veterans and those that help them, to come together and create a system that works for those struggling.

I know my story of trauma is not as bad as some Vets I have met. I was not in numerous firefights. I was not held as a POW. I was not tortured. My story may even be boring to some. So, I know there are people out there suffering worse than I did, and I can't even imagine what that is like. When I put that into perspective, it is easy to see how so many of us kill themselves each day. The question that I seek to answer is, how can we make it stop?

AFTER THOUGHT

Failure is the word pessimists give to experience. We are all going to experience some hardships through life. Times when the plan did not pan out. At these moments you have two choices. Either quit and move on or overcome and try again. I will not criticize you for either decision, because the fact of the matter is sometimes you need to drop an idea and move on because you are not meant to do it at this point in your life. There is no shame in doing what you need to do to make sure you are ok. I learned this late in the game. I went through the same cycle over and over again. I would have an idea, and it would grow along with my obsession for perfection. Mania would ensue, and I would end up losing sleep because I did not need it. This led to terrible and harmful decisions, that brought on deep depression and suicidal thoughts. Mixing this pattern with PTSD and the physical pains I have endured made waking up in the morning disappointing. It was no longer worth it to me, and I would lose a lot of productive time in my life to my ailment. This cycle did more than destroy businesses and opportunities for me. It ripped away friends and relationships that were important to me. I don't want this to be your fate.

This book is for you. The person struggling with PTSD, or the one who has a loved one struggling. I wrote this to tell you that you are not alone, and the patterns of behavior you are witnessing is typical for what you have gone through. I want you to get help but understand that it is not always easy. You don't have to dive right in. You can contact me, and we can just talk. You can share your stories with me, talk about your problems, and I will just listen. If you are ready to seek professional help, I can point you in the right direction.

If you read this and you are suffering, and you want to talk, you need to make me a promise that no matter how hard it gets you will not give up. Do not become another statistic. Instead, join with me to destroy the statistic and help our family get the recovery they deserve. I am with you. I have your 6.

Mga4278@g.rit.com